D0310041

Studying
@ University
& College

Studying @ University & College

Suzanne O'Hara

KOGAN
PAGE

YOURS TO HAVE AND TO HOLD

BUT NOT TO COPY

British Library Cataloguing in Publication Data

A CIP record for this book is available from the British Library.

ISBN 0 7494 2273 4

Typeset by Kogan Page
Printed and bound in Great Britain by
Biddles Ltd, Guilford and King's Lynn

Contents

Preface

My primary purpose in writing this book is to ensure that you learn effectively, so that you study successfully and get the most out of your years at college or university.

I have worked with many able students who, even in the final year of their course, still do not know some of the basic study skills. They find that their assessment results are not a true reflection of their real ability and have arrived at their final year the hard way. This is because many students learn how to study through trial and error, which can be a long and frustrating process. These students work very hard but may never acquire a full range of effective study skills.

I wrote this book with the idea of sharing what I have learnt over the years about effective studying. The book, therefore, is full of ideas and information, which I hope will help you be more successful in your studies and enable you to use your time effectively.

As well as giving you practical help, the book emphasizes the need for you to take responsibility for your own learning. With larger class sizes in colleges and universities, you need to be able to work more independently if you are to be successful. Your tutors are there to act as your guides in the learning process. They point you in the right direction, so you can find out about the subjects for yourself and develop your own point of view. One of the most important things that you can learn from your studies is the ability to think for yourself. I have, therefore, avoided using the word 'teacher', to emphasize the fact that you will not be 'taught' in the traditional sense of the word. Teaching is something that is done to us, learning is something we do for ourselves. You need to be active in your own learning.

Learning does not finish when your formal education comes to an end. All of us need to develop the habit of lifelong learning if we are to live successful and fulfilled lives. I hope that the skills you learn through reading and using this book will, in a small way, help you to do just that!

Suzanne O'Hara

1 *Learning to learn*

In this chapter you can:

▓ find out why learning to learn is important

▓ determine your own preferred learning style

▓ learn how to learn more effectively

Why is learning about learning important?

▓ Throughout your course of study, you need to be an independent learner. Your tutors provide a general framework, but they won't manage your learning for you. You need to work out your own priorities and motivate yourself to meet deadlines and targets.

▓ Studying will present you with different demands, at different times, for different subjects. To meet these challenges successfully, you need to be able to learn in a wide variety of ways and extend your range of learning techniques.

▓ Knowing about learning is the first step to becoming a more effective learner. If you have some insights into how you learn and know your preferred methods of learning, you will be able to make the best use of all kinds of learning opportunities.

How you learn

Learning involves understanding
If you really understand a subject, you can:

▓ remember it easily

▓ express it in your own way

▓ use what you know

Learning is an active and dynamic process
You don't learn a great deal when you just read things, or sit listening to tutors and lecturers. To learn, you need to use the material yourself, to be actively involved with it, thinking and reflecting on the ideas and concepts.

Learning occurs in fits and starts
There will be occasions when it seems as if you are making no progress. This is because learning does not happen at a uniform pace. There are usually four stages to the learning process.

Stage 1: very slow progress as you begin to become familiar with the new material
Stage 2: rapid progress as you begin to understand what the subject is all about and become more interested in it
Stage 3: slow progress as the subject becomes more difficult. You may get stuck and lose interest
Stage 4: a slow climb as you get better at the subject and begin to master it.

Not all of your learning will necessarily follow these four stages, it depends on what you are learning and your own particular circumstances. But knowing that the difficulties you are experiencing are part of the learning process and not a result of your own lack of ability can be reassuring when you are frustrated with your slow pace.

Evaluation and feedback are vital to learning
The more you evaluate your work and get feedback, the better you learn, because you:

▓ begin to realize your strengths and weaknesses

▓ develop a clearer understanding of how well you are learning

▓ develop new criteria against which to assess your learning

▓ change and adjust what you are doing

Preferred ways of learning

Learning styles

Learning theorists (Honey and Mumford, 1986) suggest that we have all developed, sometimes unconsciously, preferred methods of learning. They claim there are four different learning styles:

▓ activist

▓ reflector

▓ theorist

▓ pragmatist

To make good use of all learning opportunities, you need to be good at all four styles. However, most people are usually only good at one or two of the four styles. This means that they only learn effectively from a narrow range of learning opportunities.

Effective studying requires you to use every chance you get to maximize your learning. To do this you need to be aware of your own learning preferences and the situations where they work best. You then need to develop other ways of learning, so that you can get the most from any learning situation.

Identify your learning style

Figure 1 gives details of the different learning styles. See if you can identify your own approach to learning. Read through the descriptions below. Identify the description(s) that most closely fits you. Each style of learning works best in certain situations.

> ### Activists
> *are open minded*
>
> *enjoy the excitement of new experiences*
>
> *fill their days with activity*
>
> *problem solve by brainstorming*
>
> *move quickly from one experience to the next*
>
> *thrive on challenge*
>
> *like working with others*
>
> *like being in the centre of what is going on*
>
> ### Reflectors
> *are tolerant, calm and can seem distant*
>
> *look at experiences from many different perspectives*
>
> *enjoy collecting and analysing data*
>
> *think through information before reaching a conclusion*
>
> *put off reaching definite conclusions as long as*

possible – 'you can't have too much information'

prefer the back seat, watching and listening to others

adopt a low profile

act when they have the full picture

Theorists
tend to be detached, analytical, objective

think in a logical way and value rationality and logic

put together many different ideas into coherent theories

tend to be perfectionists

like to analyse and synthesize

are keen on assumptions, principles, theories and models

feel uncomfortable with subjective judgements, lateral thinking and anything flippant

adapt and integrate observations into complex theories

Pragmatists
are down to earth people

are impatient with too much theorizing

like making practical decisions and solving problems

like to try out ideas and theories to see if they work

search out new ideas and try them out

like to get on with things quickly

can act confidently on ideas that attract them

see problems and opportunities as a challenge

Figure 1 Learning styles

Activists learn best when:

    working in groups with other people

    involved in workshop activities

    discussing ideas with others

    working to tight deadlines

Reflectors learn best when:

    attending lectures

    doing project and research work

    working on their own

    in small group discussions

Theorists learn best when:

    reading and evaluating ideas

    questioning theory

    discussing theory with others

Pragmatists learn best when:

    involved in practical problem solving

    on work experience

    doing case studies

    taking part in workshops

How to develop your ability to learn

To develop your ability to learn you need to:

1. adopt learning strategies that fit your material

2. be an active learner

3. evaluate your work and seek feedback

1. Adopt learning strategies that fit your material

To study effectively you need to be able to get the most from all learning situations. Your *preferred* approach to learning, however, may not be the most appropriate one for every situation. Instead of relying on your old tried and tested ways of learning, you need to try out and practise new methods. Below are some suggestions about how you can do this.

Become more *Activist*:

split up your study time into half hour sections. Each half hour, change what you are doing. For example, switch from reading to mind mapping (see Chapter 6) what you have been reading, to discussing your ideas with friends

offer to lead discussion groups or make presentations

try to do something new on a regular basis

Be a better *Reflector*:

keep a learning diary, noting down the day's events and your conclusions

do some research

practise your observation and listening skills, eg at seminars and tutorials

---

Develop as a *Theorist*:

> read a 'heavy' piece of writing and summarize it in your own words

> try to pick out weaknesses in other people's arguments

> analyse a complex situation

Practise being a *Pragmatist*:

> produce study action plans

> tackle a practical project

> list uses for new ideas and techniques

2. Be an active learner

Whether you are an activist, reflector, theorist or pragmatist, you need to be active in your learning. The following are some suggestions to make your learning a more active process.

How to be an active learner

- **ask yourself questions after each lecture or after reading each chapter of a book**. For example, if there were only one thing from this that you would choose to remember, what would it be? If there were two things, what would the second one be? If there were three, what would they be?

- **draw diagrams** to illustrate concepts

- **draw pictures or cartoons** to illustrate concepts. Being able to draw well is not important. What is important is having to think about what to draw that will illustrate the concept

▧ **try to identify:**

the *strangest* concept

the *most useful* concept or idea

the *most amusing* concept or idea

the *silliest* concept or idea

the *strongest* concept or idea

the *most boring* concept or idea

▧ **keep a learning diary** about what you learned, your feelings and conclusions about how you learn

3. Evaluate your work and ask for feedback

Whether you want it or not, sooner or later you will be given feedback when your tutors evaluate and assess your work. Rather than waiting for this to happen, it is better to evaluate your own work and get feedback from other people. In this way, you have the opportunity of improving your work before you submit it for the final assessment.

Test yourself
One easy way of evaluating your learning is to test yourself. When you have completed a piece of work, set yourself questions on the material you have covered. Ask yourself: *'What could I now reasonably be expected to know/be able to do?'*. Then devise a set of questions that test how well you have got to grips with the concepts and ideas. If you test yourself regularly, you will be pleasantly surprised at how much you can remember.

Set your own learning objectives

Think about what you want to learn and then set yourself objectives for your learning. Use these objectives as criteria to evaluate how well you are learning. Compare what you have learnt with your objectives. If you have clear objectives, know your own abilities and what you have previously learned, you will be a good judge of your learning.

Ask for feedback

If you can find people on the course whom you can trust, you can work with them, share ideas and give each other feedback. You could, for example, proof read each other's work or test each other when you are revising your material. Getting feedback will enable you to find out how you are doing, by comparing your progress other people.

Start a study group

Suggest that a group of say five or six of your course members meet together regularly to give support and feedback on each other's work. People who work in groups in this way gain a great deal from being involved in other people's learning. (See Chapter 11 for how to start your own learning group.)

How to cope with negative feedback

One of the difficulties with feedback is that, in general, people tend to concentrate on what you could do better, rather than what you did well. They do this because they want you to improve and develop your skills and understanding. You need to know about the mistakes you are making so that you can correct them and get back on track. This does not mean you will enjoy hearing about your mistakes. If people are giving you negative feedback, try not to get defensive. You don't have to explain or justify or retaliate. All you need to do is listen. Try not to focus on the mistakes themselves, instead concentrate on how you can correct them.

To get a more balanced view, when you ask for feedback on your written work from friends, suggest they tell you:

▓ three things they would like more of

▓ three things they would like less of

▓ three things that could stay the same

Or you could ask them to give you feedback about your strengths as well as your weaknesses. In this way, you get feedback on all aspects of your work, not just the negative things. When people give you positive feedback, don't be tempted to discount it or shrug it off. You need all their feedback to help you progress your learning.

Learning to learn: key points

▓ Recognize and develop your own learning style.

▓ Be active in your learning.

▓ Develop your ability to evaluate your own work.

▓ Ask for positive and negative feedback.

Reference

Honey, P. and Mumford, A., *Using Your Learning Styles*, Maidenhead, Pete Honey Publications, 1986.

2 *Managing yourself*

In this chapter you can:

▨ learn how to motivate yourself

▨ get ideas about planning your time and getting organized

▨ find ways to manage your stress

▨ discover where to go to find help and support

Motivating yourself

Your reasons for wanting to study play an important part in being a successful learner. Studying is demanding! You need good reasons for doing it; reasons that will act as your driving force and keep you motivated. If you know why you are studying, you are more likely to be able to weather the rough patches.

Determine your own motives for studying
These may include some of the following:

▨ improved career prospects

▨ gaining an educational qualification for a higher level course

▨ learning more about a subject

▨ developing your mind

▨ widening your horizons

※ proving to yourself and others that you can complete a degree

Keep a record of your long-term goals and your reasons for starting out on the course. When things get difficult, rereading them may help get you remotivated. You could also meet and talk through your plans with a friend or a member of your family. Report back to them regularly on your progress.

Set targets and goals

Setting targets and goals helps keep you motivated and gets you in the right frame of mind for learning and studying. It is important to set yourself both long and short-term goals because:

※ if you have a clear idea of where you are going, you are more likely to get there

※ it is satisfying to measure your progress to your overall goal

※ breaking large tasks into small manageable chunks means that they are less daunting: you make molehills out of mountains

Make your goals realistic

To set goals you need to make a realistic appraisal of how you have performed in the past, so that you can predict how you will perform in the future. You also need to have an understanding of your own ability, so that you can estimate what is realistic for you to achieve. There is no point in setting goals that are impossible to achieve. If you do, you will only end up feeling a failure when the inevitable happens and you don't achieve them.

Sometimes we overestimate our ability to get work done, so when you have set your goals it is a good idea to get other people's views. It might, for example, seem realistic to you to do all the revision for your examinations in a few days. To test how realistic this is as a goal, ask your friends and other members of your course. Rewrite the goals if necessary in the light of their feedback.

Planning your time

On most courses, it seems as if you have a great deal of 'free' time. You may, for example, only attend classes for between 12 and 18 hours a week. Although you may be given work that you have to prepare for your next class, it is more likely that you will be given assignments to be done over a number of weeks.

At first sight, it might seem as if you have very little to do in the way of studying. This is not the case. You are expected to put in a considerable amount of time in private study. It is not part of the tutors' role to see that you complete the private study part of the course. They will just assess the results. They expect **you** to plan and organize your time for yourself.

Planning when and how you are going to use your time ensures that you use it in the most productive way. It also minimizes the stress that results from having to complete work at the last minute. How you choose to do this planning is up to you. You need to know yourself and how you work best.

Study timetables

One way of planning your time is to write out timetables. Timetables have a number of benefits. They:

§ give you a target to aim for

§ spread out your study

§ help to establish a routine

❋ encourage you to keep up

❋ save time in decision making

1. A year plan

Filling in a year plan will enable you to see, on a single sheet, all your assessment target dates, your examinations, holidays and other commitments. You will also be able to see where your heavy periods of work occur. Knowing this in advance makes it easier to structure your study for the whole year.

At the start of the academic year, find out what assessed and non assessed work you are required to do. You may need to keep checking that you have a complete set of the course requirements and that you have not left anything out. Estimate how long you need to spend on each piece of work. You should also find out the dates of your examinations and allow time to do your revision.

Write out a year plan including all the information that you have collected. Keep the year plan where you can see it, for example on your wall or your desk.

2. Weekly timetables

Writing out a weekly study timetable requires some self-knowledge, since you need to know how and when you learn best. For example, are your best times for studying in the early morning, late at night or in the afternoon? Do you work best in the library, with other people, or on your own?

Allow time for:

❋ attending classes

❋ working on lecture notes

❋ reading and note-making

❋ researching, visiting the library

❋ writing assessed pieces of work

▓ editing

▓ rest and relaxation!

What is a 'reasonable' length of time for a study session?

You can only maintain concentration for a limited amount of time, so don't plan long study sessions without taking breaks. The work you are doing determines how long the study session should be. Tackling something new may need a long period, other tasks, like going over work you already understand, may take much shorter periods of time.

A good deal of research suggests that periods of 40–50 minutes are best for concentration and memory. After this time, you need to take a break. It's a good idea to vary the work that you do in a study session. For example, beginning some new work and then practising things that are familiar to you.

Review your timetable at intervals in the light of your experience of studying and according to the changing demands of your course. You may find, for example, that it would be better for you to allow time to work in the early morning, rather than late at night when you have been too tired to concentrate. Reflect on how well you are able to achieve your targets. You might need to have fewer long sessions and more, shorter ones. Adjust your timetable as necessary.

What if you fall behind your timetable?

Keeping to your timetable is not always easy. If you fall behind, or seem to be constantly reorganizing your time, don't worry. At least you are still thinking strategically about what you are doing and not just floating along with the tide. The more you practise, the better you will become at time management.

3. Other ways to plan your time

You may not like working to a detailed plan and prefer a more open approach. If this is the case, you still need to set aside times each week for study or you will find assessment deadlines looming with too little time to complete your work.

Set a weekly target for your study time

You will be more productive if you discipline yourself to work at set times during the week and work regularly throughout the year. What you are aiming for is to set aside certain hours for study and to plan to do some studying each week. Don't be tempted to take things easy in the first part of the year and then cram everything into the last part of it. If you do this, your work is likely to suffer. You will not do yourself justice and you are likely to subject yourself to undue stress.

If you have set times for study, it will make it easier to get down to work. You won't waste time trying to decide when to study.

How you use the time depends on the work that you are doing. It is useful if you keep a weekly record of your study time, to ensure that you are meeting your target hours.

Write weekly 'to do' lists

A 'to do' list is a very simple way of organizing your time. Write out a list of all your study tasks and decide when you are going to do them. As they are completed, cross them off your list. At the beginning of each week, write out a new 'to do' list. Carry over any items from the previous week's list that you have not yet completed.

Using your study time

Before you begin a study session, go through in your mind the work that you want to get done. Doing this will help you get in the right frame of mind for the task in hand.

Set yourself targets and goals at the start of the session. Write down what you plan to learn in the time available. Effective studying is not about how long you study or at what times, it's about getting through what you need to, in the time available. When you meet your target, reward yourself!

Start working straight away, but begin slowly and easily and build up as the session progresses. It is a good idea to start each study session by recalling what you studied last time, then move on to the new area of work.

Take breaks during your study period. They will help you maintain your level of concentration and aid study. When you take your breaks is up to you. A break after 20–40 minutes' studying is a rough guide. At the end of each study session take a break, then review the information you have covered. This helps you to remember it for longer.

Getting organized

Being organized saves both your time and your nerves. It is frustrating wasting precious time looking for the notes that you made last week or trying to remember the name of the book you read a while ago that you now need for your next piece of work. You need to:

1. organize your study area, and
2. organize your notes and materials

1. Your study area

Somewhere that is quiet and free from distraction is essential for studying. If you can, it is a good idea to try to work in the same place all the time. Associating a particular place with study means that, as you make your way there, you are already getting your mind into study mode. When you arrive you settle down more quickly.

You study better if you are comfortable and relaxed, but not too relaxed! Consider things like the lighting level of your study area, its ventilation and the furniture. You are going to be doing a considerable amount of studying, so it's worth spending some time getting these things right.

If it is not possible for you to have a study area that is undisturbed, you may find it easier to work in a library. Seeing other people working sometimes makes it easier to get down to work yourself. The library will also have rules about not talking, which should help you concentrate. It may even have individual study cubicles that you can use, so you are not distracted by people moving about.

Remember also:

▓ **You can do some studying wherever you are**, you don't always have to be in your study area. Revising material that you have already covered can be done almost anywhere.

▓ **You don't need all your materials round you to study.**

▓ **You only need your brain to think!**

2. Organizing your notes and materials

You will build up a considerable amount of notes from lectures and reading. You will also have handouts from the course and work for your assessments. You therefore need to keep these in an organized way, using a system that can expand as your materials grow.

To organize your materials, you need:

▩ pocket files

▩ ring binders

▩ subject dividers

▩ box files

▩ a box of index cards

▩ shelf space

It is a good idea to arrange your notes thematically. Once you have established your themes, you then need to file the notes. Do this roughly at first; you can always rearrange your notes as the themes become clearer. Filing is part of the process of revision. As you file your notes, you have to glance at them to decide which category they belong to, this helps you remember them. It is also easy to find notes when you need them.

Organize the material contained in them. Don't just organize and file your notes. You will be able to learn more easily if you do this in as many different ways as possible. For example:

▩ draw mind maps (see Chapter 6)

▩ use plans, pictures, cartoons or diagrams to illustrate concepts

▩ use your lecture notes to construct a flow chart outline of the course

Managing your stress

Stress is a normal part of living, but it can have positive or negative effects. Too much stress will affect your thinking, your emotions and your behaviour. Therefore you need to be able to manage your stress levels if you are going to study effectively.

It is not so much events themselves which determine whether you are stressed or not, as your reactions to them. Problems with stress occur when there is an imbalance between the demands that are made on you and your resources for coping with these demands.

The first step in managing stress is to develop your awareness of your own stress pattern. Try to answer the following questions:

1. *What things do you find particularly stressful?*

2. *In what ways does stress affect your:*

    thinking

    body

    emotions

    social life

    behaviour

Having answered these questions, you should begin to become aware of your sources of stress and how stress affects you. Once you are aware of this, you can watch out for your own signs of stress, monitor your stress levels and take action before you are too badly affected by it.

Ways of reducing your stress

Take care of your health:

- eat regular, well balanced meals
- cut down on your caffeine and alcohol intake
- get enough sleep

- take cat-naps if you can't sleep at night
- practise deep breathing and relaxation techniques
- do some physical exercise, even a brisk walk can be beneficial

Manage your work:

- work with other students on your most difficult subject areas. See if you can share out some of the tasks that you need to complete
- talk through your worry with a friend
- talk to your tutor
- start working rather than just worrying about it
- split large, seemingly impossible tasks into small, achievable pieces

Overcoming problems

As the course progresses, you may find it more difficult to keep yourself motivated and up to date with your work. The following are some suggestions to help you cope with some of the problems you may encounter.

Problem: getting discouraged because the work is difficult
If you find the work itself difficult, there may be a number of reasons for this:

- You could have reached a learning plateau and need a period of consolidation before you go on.
- You may not have been learning as efficiently and thoroughly as you thought; a period of revision might help.
- You may need to take more breaks in your study time to keep you fresh.

※ You may have set yourself unrealistic targets; review them and rewrite them if necessary.

※ You may need to discuss the work with one of your tutors.

Problem: you keep putting things off

※ Work on your motivation. Keep reminding yourself of what's in it for you. Look forward to the benefits that come with success. If you are able to see a purpose for your studying, rather than just feeling that you ought to study, you'll have less trouble with procrastination.

※ Do your studying in small chunks. As you complete each step, you will build up momentum.

※ Make a list of the tasks that you have completed as evidence of your progress.

※ Get into the habit of doing some study each day.

※ Let other people know your targets and your problem. The fact that someone else will be asking you if you completed that assignment you talked about yesterday, is a strong motivator.

Problem: you get bored

※ Get interested in your studies; remind yourself of your reasons for studying.

※ Set yourself realistic targets. Don't expect miracles.

※ Take breaks and get some exercise.

Problem: you fall behind your targets

※ List the reasons that caused you to fall behind. Then write out ways to avoid the same things happening again.

▨ Review your timetable. It may not be as realistic as you thought.

▨ The work may have been more difficult than you had allowed for. In future build in emergency time on your timetable so that you have some spare for such occasions.

Where to get help

A variety of services are provided offering you advice, guidance and information.

Personal tutors

At the start of your course, you will usually be allocated a personal tutor. Your tutor is someone you can approach about any personal, domestic, financial or academic problem. As well as being a source of help and support, your personal tutor will be asked to write your academic references when you apply for jobs. If your tutor does not know you very well, your reference will be based mainly on your assessment results and your attendance record. You will get a more in-depth reference if you spend time getting to know your tutor.

You should meet with your personal tutor at least once each semester. At the first meeting, make your personal tutor aware of any special needs you have or particular assistance that you need, for example, if you are dyslexic or if you have hearing problems.

If, during the year, you have personal problems or practical problems with housing, finances, your family, etc, your personal tutor will normally be the first person you go to. Most tutors try to be understanding. They may not always be able to give you advice or answer all your questions, but they will know who can provide different types of specialist support and be able to refer you to other services.

Careers

The careers adviser can give you advice on choosing the right course and option subjects, changing courses, further study, applying for jobs including part-time and vacation work, writing CVs and interview skills.

Counselling

The student counselling service is usually available to all students, including those living at home. The service normally provides one-to-one counselling sessions in a private and confidential setting. It may also have confidential telephone helplines so you can talk with trained staff. There may also be occasional workshops on subjects like stress management and coping with exam anxiety.

Counsellors are familiar with the range of problems that can occur during your studies. For example you might become involved in a dispute with the owner of your flat; you may feel that you are being subjected to sexual harassment; you may have serious family problems; or you may get into legal difficulties. You may have worries about your ability to get through the course successfully, or to acknowledge that you are not succeeding in an activity when you believe you should be. The aim of counselling is to help you clarify your thoughts and feelings so that you can arrive at your own decisions. The counsellor will therefore help you to talk through your concerns and not judge you or tell you what to do.

Medical services

There is usually a student health centre run on campus. It is probably in a convenient location and will be staffed by people who understand student pressures and problems. The centre provides medical advice and treatment. You will also be able to get information about how to register with a local doctor.

Student union

To make use of the student union, you need to be a member. You usually automatically become a member when you enrol for your course. The union represents students on all the main decision making committees, so that the student viewpoint can be taken into consideration. It also provides an advisory service for all its members. The union probably has facilities to help you if you have legal or financial problems, or problems with your accommodation. The union may also be able to offer help with other kinds of problems and, if not, is likely to have leaflets and handouts on a wide range of subjects.

Welfare and financial advice

Most institutions provide a service where you can get advice about financial problems. You will be able to get information and advice about loans, student concessions and, in an emergency, they may be able to arrange an interest-free loan.

Friends and self help groups

Do not forget the importance of developing a network of friends who can provide support. Talk about your problems with your friends on your course and encourage them to talk to you about theirs. Form self-help learning groups with other students on your course so that you can make new friends and gain from each other's experience, interests and abilities (see Chapter 11).

Managing yourself: key points

- Keep yourself motivated.
- Set goals and targets for your studies and regularly assess your progress.
- Plan your study time.
- Organize your notes and materials.
- Monitor your own stress levels.
- Identify places you can go to get help.

3 *Starting a new subject*

This chapter offers you information and ideas to help you:

▓ find out about the subject you are taking

▓ understand what is expected of you as a student

▓ understand different assessment procedures

▓ work with your tutors

You will only receive a limited amount of guidance when beginning a new subject. You need therefore to be prepared to approach a wide range of people and ask them for advice and help. You may, for example, have to ask questions of a professor you have not spoken to before; seek help from a member of staff you see only once a week; put forward your own thoughts in a seminar; make contact with a stranger sitting next to you in a class. It will take time to develop the necessary skills and you need to be prepared to take risks.

Finding out about a new subject

Each subject has a particular way of operating with its own language and subject vocabulary, so from the start you need to become familiar with how things are done.

The academic year

Within the year, periods of study are divided into a number of different units.

▓ **Semesters:** there are two semesters in the academic year. Each semester lasts approximately 15 weeks, with assessments and exams at the end of the semester. In practice, this means that you are often expected to start a new subject and reach the required standard, in only 15 weeks.

▓ **Vacations** are times when there are no classes and you are not required to attend. Vacations, however, are not always *holidays*. You may have to use them to complete coursework.

▓ **Reading week:** during this time, classes do not take place and you are expected to complete assessed work, catch up on your reading, etc. Some subjects schedule field trips and other off campus activities during this week.

▓ **Revision weeks** may be timetabled for the end of each semester to enable you to prepare for your examinations. Sometimes members of staff hold revision classes during revision weeks and these are well worth attending.

The first session

Your new subject will probably begin with an introductory session. At this session, the subject you are studying may be described using some of the following terms:

▓ **Units or modules:** self-contained subjects, which last for one semester. Marks for these units may count towards your final degree.

▓ **Core units or core modules:** compulsory units. In some courses all the units may be compulsory, in others you may be able to choose most of your units from a list of choices.

▓ **Options or electives:** units you can choose to take or not. There will be a minimum number of options you are required to undertake. The more flexible your course, the more options units you have, but the more choices you have to make yourself.

▒ **Prerequisites:** units you need to have passed before you can enrol for other units. You may also need to study certain subjects if you have a particular career in mind. You can get information about such prerequisites from a careers office or a library.

▒ **Corequisites:** two or more units that need to be studied at the same time.

▒ **Exam boards:** meetings of tutors to discuss and agree all your assessment marks. Exam boards usually take place following the end of each semester.

Sources of information

The syllabus

The main source of information you will be given is the syllabus. This usually contains some or all of the following information:

▒ **Subject aims:** an overview of the subject area.

▒ **Learning outcomes:** what you should have learnt by the time you have completed the subject.

▒ **Content:** details of the different topics that are included in this subject. The word *indicative* is sometimes included to show that this list of topics is only suggested, not fixed. This means that some of the topics may not be covered.

▒ **Lecture programme:** an outline of the topics to be covered in lectures and the weeks when each topic will be covered.

▒ **Preparation:** reading you are expected to complete for each lecture, seminar and tutorial.

▒ **Assessment:** details of the assessments you are required to take at the end of the subject.

▓ **Reading:** a list of the recommended reading materials. This may include a set textbook, books and journal articles. (See Chapter 8 for more details.)

The Intranet
This is a computerized database about your institution. If your institution has one, it may include the following information:

The course in general:

▓ on line course notice boards

▓ student handbooks, university regulations, etc

▓ course and examination timetables

▓ email links to course administrators, lecturers and tutors

▓ course material

Subject information:

▓ assignment and assessment schedules

▓ reading lists, links to other useful web sites

▓ past exam papers

▓ teaching resources

▓ on line discussion groups for each subject, which may be based around the work done in seminars and tutorials

▓ Internet research tips

General:

▓ links to the library catalogues

▓ links to staff research papers

Contact the computer technicians or the library staff for information about how to access the Intranet.

What is expected of you

You are expected to manage your own work and study and to fulfil the formal requirements for your subject. The formal requirements usually include:

▓ attendance

▓ completing assessments

▓ meeting assessment deadlines

Attendance

You need to find out what the requirements are for attendance at lectures, tutorials and seminars. You may find that there is no formal requirement for you to attend lectures, but you may be penalized if you do not attend seminars and tutorials since assessment may be linked to them.

Remember also that if you attend all your classes, the members of staff get to know you; they are therefore able to talk about you at examination boards. This is especially useful if you have borderline marks. If you are relatively unknown because of your poor attendance record, they are much less able to do this.

Completing assessments

You will be expected to complete pieces of work so that your progress in the subject can be assessed. There are a number of different types of assessments.

Time constrained assessments

These can take a variety of forms:

▓ **Traditional examinations:** when you work on an unseen paper for between one and three hours.

▓ **Take away examinations:** in advance of the examination, you collect a text which you take away. During the examination you are required to answer unseen questions on that text and sometimes to work with additional unseen material. How far in advance of the exam you collect the text can vary from between 24 hours to two weeks.

▓ **Open book examinations:** allow you to take a variety of materials into the examination, eg texts, course notes or your own notes on the text. You may even be given the examination questions in advance.

▓ **Short answer examinations:** a large number of questions are set. You are required to answer these questions briefly in a single word, sentence or short paragraph.

▓ **Multiple choice examinations:** a large number of questions are set and you choose your answer from a limited number of choices, for example one answer from six suggested answers.

(See Chapter 13 for a more detailed explanation.)

Course work

Written course work is usually an essential part of your course of study. In many cases course work counts towards your final degree classification. Course work may take the form of:

▓ **written assignments,** for example essays, case studies, laboratory reports, business reports, seminar papers and presentations

▓ **project work** where you choose an area of special interest, do research and write up a project report

▓ **a dissertation:** a substantial piece of work usually done in your final year. This involves choosing your own subject, setting out your central question, working out your methodology, carrying out research, analysing and writing up the results

Group work

Some course work may be conducted in small groups. You may be required to:

▓ write a group assignment or report

▓ make a presentation

Usually all group members share the grades for group work and are therefore held jointly responsible for the standard and quality of the work.

Assessment results

Your assessments may be given marks or grades, or they may be classified in the same way as your final degree. In the UK degree classifications are as follows:

▓ first class: 70 per cent or over

▓ upper second class: 60–69 per cent

▓ lower second class: 50–59 per cent

▓ third class: 40–49 per cent

▓ pass: 35–39 per cent

▓ fail: 0–34 per cent

Even if you gain more than 40 per cent, if you fail to meet certain criteria, you may only be awarded a pass degree. Not all your assessed work automatically goes towards this final classification. Check with your tutors to find out which assessments count towards your final degree.

Retaking assessments

If you have failed an assessment, you need to find out if it is possible for you to retake it. Policies about retakes vary from course to course. For example, on some courses you may only be able to retake the assessment once. On other courses, you can do as many retakes as you like. There may, however, be an upper limit on the mark you can be awarded for a retake.

Formal appeals

If you have any serious problems with exams or assessments, procedures exist for you to make a formal appeal to senior members of staff about what took place. These procedures will normally be detailed in the university handbook. The kind of circumstances that may lead you to make a formal appeal would be, for example, if there were questions on your exam paper that covered areas that were not on the syllabus.

Meeting assessment deadlines

It is your responsibility to submit work on time. The dates for submission of course work may be in the details you are given at the start of a new subject.

Each piece of course work will have a *latest submission date* by which the work must be completed. Make sure you hand your work in before the deadline expires. For some subjects, the assessed mark is reduced for every working day that the assignment is late. Typically this means that for each day late, you lose 5 per cent of the overall mark. Even if you are only 5 minutes after the deadline, expect to lose marks. Sometimes your work will not be marked at all, if, for example, it is handed in more than 10 days after the deadline.

If you are experiencing difficulties in meeting the deadlines, it is advisable to inform your personal tutor and subject tutor before the due date. If you have to hand in work after the deadline, you need to provide a written explanation of the reason for the late submission. If you have been ill, most members of staff will usually react sympathetically, but they will require documentary evidence of your illness, for example a doctor's letter. Computer failure is not normally accepted as a justification for a late hand-in. Therefore, aim to complete with a day or two to spare, in order to make good any work you lose.

Working with your tutors

Subject tutors play an important part in your learning. However, sometimes students are not clear about the role of tutors and therefore have unrealistic expectations about how their tutors should behave. The tutors' job is not to tell you all you need to know. They are not information bearers who deliver learning to you ready packaged. You need to be responsible for producing your own learning. Tutors are there to act as your guides in the learning process. They point you in the right direction and provide signposts, so that you can find out about the subject for yourself and develop your own point of view.

Tutors are an important resource that you can use to increase your learning. Don't forget, however, that they are also human and like to be treated as such! Although they are a resource, don't treat them like a library book which you pick up when you feel like it, take what you want and then put down.

Remember that tutors do more than just take classes
Face to face teaching is only one part of a tutor's job. They are also expected to:

▓ read to keep up to date with their subject

▓ research

▓ do administration

▓ write books

▓ attend conferences

▓ be involved in course development

▓ attend meetings and sit on committees

▓ counsel students

Don't be offended or surprised therefore if tutors are sometimes less willing to spend time chatting with you than you would like. If you want to speak to them, make an appointment. Many tutors have weekly 'surgery hours', when they have set time aside to see students.

Attend all classes
Attend all the sessions so that you can get every bit of information that may be useful to you. If you have to miss a class, tell the tutor in advance. When you miss a class and don't explain why, you are conveying a message to your tutor that you don't value what they are saying. If you don't like the tutor, you should still attend the class. You don't have to like people in order to be able to learn from them.

If you are having serious problems with a tutor, for example because of harassment, there are complaints procedures that you can follow. These procedures will be detailed in the university handbook.

Turn up on time
Everyone concerned is affected if you are late. You will miss part of the class and other people will be disturbed when you come in. If it is inevitable that you will be late, tell the tutor the reason for this in advance.

Don't be put off if the tutor doesn't know your name

Most tutors will want to get to know you as a person, but, many teach a hundred or more different students each week. As class sizes get larger, even the most willing tutor is less likely to be able to get to know each student personally. Some tutors are shy outside the classroom or are private people who prefer to relate to their students through the subject rather than becoming personally involved.

Be prepared to ask questions

Most tutors enjoy talking with students who want to learn. They usually appreciate students whose questions and comments show genuine thought and enthusiasm for learning. If you have difficulties in a subject, most tutors would prefer you to seek advice or assistance from them rather than keeping quiet about it.

If you are nervous about asking a question, it might help you to remember that if you don't know the answer, it is likely that other people don't know it either. You are probably doing everyone a service by asking the question. If you don't manage to ask your question during the class, you can always ask it at the end of the class.

Starting a new subject: key points

▓ Become familiar with the subject's language and way of working.

▓ Find out what is required from you in terms of attendance and assessment.

▓ Develop a good working relationship with your tutors.

---

4 Using the library

This chapter helps you to:

▓ find your way round the library

▓ locate the texts you need

▓ use electronic sources of information

▓ do research

The library of an academic institution can appear daunting to new students. To begin with, libraries are big, often needing several complete buildings to house the different collections. They may also seem livelier than you expect, with large numbers of people moving around. They may also be noisier than you expect, although the library staff do their best to keep down noise levels.

In the course of your studies, you will be a frequent visitor to the library. It is a rich source of information, so it is important that you become familiar with how to use it effectively. To do this you need to know the general layout of the library and understand how to get access to the information that you want.

Finding your way round the library

The library offers much more in the way of information sources than simply books. In addition to thousands of books, the following may also be available:

- **journals, periodicals** which contain original and review articles on a wide range of subjects. Current issues are usually on display. Back issues may be on the shelves or available on CD-ROM or microfilm

- **access to the Internet**, email and electronic databases

- **CD-ROMs** which provide information on articles in journals and newspapers. Although many are simply indexes, some provide the full text of the article. Other CD-ROMs hold bibliographical and statistical databases and other reference sources including encyclopaedias and newspapers

- **audio and video tapes and equipment** relating to a wide range of subjects. The library may also have playback facilities for the video and audio collections

- **multi-media self teaching packs**

- **copies of past examination papers**

- **government publications** such as reports, year books and manuals

- **photographic, photocopying, fax and telex services**

- **Inter-library loans:** if the material you need is not in stock in the library, you can usually apply for an inter-library loan. This means that the book will be borrowed from another library for you. It may, however, take a number of weeks before your book arrives. There will also usually be a limit to the number of requests for inter-library loans you can make

Learning how to use the library

Visits to the library are usually organized for you. Don't be tempted to skip the visit. The small amount of time you spend being introduced to the library facilities will be rewarded when you begin using the library. During the visit you should find out:

▓ how the library is set out

▓ where things are kept

▓ how to access the information you need

▓ the general operating procedures, for example how to borrow books and other items, how to make reservations

▓ how to book resources, for example the computing facilities

Part of the visit may involve completing a library workbook. This is well worth doing. You will learn more about the facilities if you try them for yourself, than you will if you are simply told what to do by a member of the library staff.

Don't rely on there being a member of staff nearby whenever you need help. You will probably have to queue at the information desk to get advice, so the more self reliant you can be the more time you will save. During the visit, make sure you get copies of any maps and publications describing the library's layout and operation. Also check if there are instruction sheets for using the other services, for example the CD-ROMs.

Things you need to find out during the visit

The layout of the library

▓ *where you get a library card. You will need to take it with you each time you want to borrow books*

▓ *where you can find help. There will be an enquiry desk staffed by a member of the library staff who will usually be able to answer your questions*

▓ *where to find your subject specialist. If you have complicated questions, you may be referred to the member of the library staff who specializes in your subject area, so you will need to know where the person is located*

▓ if there is a computer pool in the library and where it is, and whether the pool opening hours are the same as those of the library. Some computer pools have longer opening times

▓ where you can find the nearest food, drink and lavatories

▓ whether there are special rooms for group work

▓ where the photocopiers are located, what form of payment they take

▓ where audio and video tapes are stored

▓ which CD-ROMs are available and where they are kept

How the library operates

▓ what the opening hours are during term time and vacation time

▓ how the cataloguing system works

▓ what the various loan times are for books and journals

▓ how many books you can have out at any one time

▓ what the penalties are if you return your books late

▓ if you can renew an item by 'phone, post or whether it has to be done in person

▓ whether all books have to be returned at the end of the summer term. This is usually done to make sure that you can account for all the books on your library record

How a library is organized

Subjects are given a classification number or letter and books are classified according to their subject. The shelves are arranged in order of their classification number or letter. There are two main classification systems:

1. The Dewey decimal system

This is the system most commonly used in libraries in the UK. It uses 10 broad classes of subject for the main branches of knowledge. For example:

000 General topics

100 Philosophy and Psychology

200 Religion

300 Social sciences

and so on

Each broad class has 10 subdivisions. For example:

300 Social sciences

310 Statistics

320 Political science

330 Economics

and so on

Each subdivision is also divided up and numbers are then given to all the related subjects that come under the subdivision. (See Appendix A for further details.) In this way a book on any given subject can be classified exactly within its general group. It is worth familiarizing yourself with the Dewey numbers attached to your subject.

2. The Library of Congress System

This uses letters to identify 21 broad subject areas. For example:

A Encyclopaedias and reference books

B Philosophy, Psychology, Religion

C *Antiquities, Biography*

D *History*

etc

A second letter is used to show subdivision within each class. For example:

Q *Science*

QA *Mathematics*

QB *Astronomy*

QC *Physics*

Further subdivisions are made by adding numbers to the initial letter. (See Appendix B for further details.)

Special categories

In addition to classifying books according to their subject, librarians use other criteria to divide up the book collection.

- **Reference books:** the reference collection contains encyclopaedias, dictionaries, atlases, etc. These items are for dipping into rather than for reading and so are not available for loan outside the library.

- **Short loan:** some books are issued on a short loan, which means, because the books are very popular, the borrowing period will be less than for ordinary books.

- **Overnight loans:** these may only be taken out just before the library's closing time. They must be returned at opening time the next day.

- **Desk/popular loans:** books and journals in heavy demand will be kept in a special collection and are usually only available by asking a member of the library staff. They may only be used in the library or taken out on an overnight loan. You may need to book a time to get access to these books and the access may be limited to a period of anything from half an hour to two hours.

▓ **Oversized books and small pamphlets** are often shelved together at the beginning or end of a subject section.

Finding books and other items

Using the catalogues
You can find details of all the books, journals and videotapes in the library by using the computer catalogues, these are called **OPACs, (on-line public access catalogues)**. The OPAC is a computerized catalogue showing details of all the materials held within the library. It enables you to locate items by giving you their classification numbers. The OPAC will also show you if an item is out on loan, enable you to make reservations and also inspect your own borrowing record.

The details of how the OPAC system works differ from library to library. Most programs, however, are likely to begin with a **menu** showing the different ways you can use the catalogue to search for specific items. There will probably also be functions to:

▓ provide more help on using the catalogue

▓ reserve a book

▓ search for other books on the same subject by the same author

▓ find out more about the title you are looking at

▓ start a new search

How to use the catalogues to search for:

▓ **Books**: if you are looking for a book which is recommended on your reading list, you will already have been given the name of the author and its title. In this case you need to select **Author** and **Title** from the search menu and find its classification number. From this number you will be able to work out on which shelf the book is stored. It will also tell you if the book is out on loan and, if so, when it is due back.

▓ **Periodicals, journals and magazines**: you will be asked to read articles from periodicals, journals and magazines. To find them in the catalogue, you need to select **Title** from the menu and use the title of the journal to begin your search.

▓ **By subject**: you will often need to do background reading for an assignment. To find books on a particular topic when you do not have the name of an author or title, start your search by selecting **Subject**. You can also search using **keywords** to locate material that might be useful.

▓ **Videotapes and other media items**: audio and video tapes are treated in exactly the same way as books. You can either find them by selecting **Title** or by looking under their subject's **classification number**.

Once you have obtained the classification number from the catalogue, you can work out on which shelf the item is stored. Note down the whole number from the catalogue, it will help you find the exact location of the item.

What if the item is missing from the shelf?

If you find the exact location and the item you are looking for is not there, scan the shelves around the spot where the item should be. Previous readers are sometimes rather careless when reshelving items. They put things back in *generally* the area, but not *exactly* in the right place.

If the book is not on nearby shelves, there are a number of things you can do. Check to see if the item is:

▓ out on loan

▓ in a special collection

▓ at the desk waiting to be reshelved

If you do not succeed in tracking down the item, check again the following day. If it is still not there, it is possible that it has been accidentally mis-shelved or deliberately mis-shelved, so that no-one else can find it. It may even have been stolen. You should notify the library staff if, after a number of attempts, you fail to locate an item that the OPAC indicates is not out on loan.

Locating journals and periodicals

Journal and _periodical_ are terms given to specialist academic magazines. These publications keep readers up to date with what is going on in a particular subject area. Each issue includes several articles and most articles are usually preceded by an abstract. In the abstract the main points of the article are summarized in a few words.

Journals are usually issued several times a year and publishers use a variety of ways to identify each issue. The most commonly used method is the **volume and number system**. All issues published within a specified period of time, usually one year, are part of the same volume. Within a volume, each issue is given a different number. In addition, all journals show the year of publication and many of them also show the month of publication. For example:

Harvard Business Review 98, Volume 76, Number 1, January–February 1998

Harvard Business Review 98, Volume 76, Number 2, March–April 1998

The library often has a special area to display current issues of journals. The journals are arranged either alphabetically by title, or by using the library's standard classification system. When a new issue is published, the previous issue is stored with the rest of the back copies of the journal. In some libraries all journals are shelved together in a special collection; in others, journals are shelved along with the books according to subject classification. Individual issues making up a complete volume are often bound in a hard cover.

It may be possible to borrow journals, if they are not the most recent copies. Complete bound volumes are usually not available for loan.

Indexes and abstracts

These journals list articles by subject and so they can help you discover what articles on a particular subject have been published in a range of journals. There are two types of referencing journal:

▮ **indexing journals** which list the author, title and journal details. These journals tend to cover a wide range of subjects

▮ **abstracting journals** which, in addition to the above, also provide an abstract or summary of each article

Using electronic sources of information

Access to electronic sources of information is usually available as part of the facilities offered through the library. Electronic databases give you access to a wide range of references. For example:

▮ books

▮ periodical articles

▓ theses

▓ conference proceedings

▓ reports

▓ book reviews

They can make searching for material faster and potentially more effective than ever before. While traditional printed indexes or abstracts often limit you to searching under Author, Title or Subject, electronic sources usually allow you to:

▓ search any term in the database

▓ link search terms

▓ refine your search in a variety of ways so that you can decide how broad or narrow to make it

Electronic services provide information such as:

▓ complete publications in full text on CD-ROM, for example, *The Oxford English Dictionary*

▓ statistical data, company information and pictures

▓ full text articles together with a full indexing and abstracting service

▓ tables of contents from periodicals, with no other data added. These offer fairly basic search facilities, but have the advantage of being very up-to-date and usually large in size

Different databases use different search conventions. Before starting a search, spend a few minutes reading any introductory guide provided or using the 'Help' screens which are usually available on the databases themselves. Heavy demand may make it advisable to book in advance for access to the CD-ROM, for example.

For some subjects, printed index and abstracting services may still be more relevant than electronic sources, especially if you need references going back many years.

The Internet

You may be able to access the Internet via the library. It is accessed using a variety of tools depending on your purpose. These purposes can include:

※ sending messages (email)

※ taking part in discussions (Usenet)

※ transferring software (ftp)

※ finding information (World Wide Web/Gopher)

Access to the Internet

In order to access the Internet, you will probably need to register with the computer centre. Students in universities and colleges usually have Internet access which is *free at the point of use*. You will therefore only have to pay if you want to dial in to the network from where you live. There will be some restrictions on your use of the Internet, for example about file storage space, so it is a good idea to find out what these restrictions are when you register.

Locating information

Although there is a vast amount of information to be found on the Internet, because the Internet has very little structure or indexing, **useful** information can be difficult to find. However tools for information retrieval are developing all the time. The computer centre will advise you about ways of making your Internet use more efficient and effective.

Using material from the Internet for assessed work

Many published books and articles have gone through a process of evaluation by other experts in the field. Resources originating from the Internet have not gone through a similar process. Any information you find on the Internet is only as good as the provider makes it. It is important therefore to be critical of the information you find. Consider whether it is accurate, comprehensive and up to date. Learning to distinguish between facts and opinions is crucial when using information found on the Internet. (See Chapter 10 for how to reference Internet material.)

Using the library for research

At some stage in your course of study, you will probably be asked to research a topic as part of a project or assignment. The following suggests a logical route for using the library to find information.

1. **Understand the question:** use general dictionaries and encyclopaedias to help you with basic terms. Look up technical words and phrases in a specialist dictionary.

2. **Do some background reading:** this usually requires you to read about the topic in relevant textbooks.

3. **Find the facts and figures:** locate and collect existing data. Most of the data will be in the Reference section of the library.

4. **Find the latest information:** this usually appears in the form of newspaper or journal articles.

5. **Search electronic databases:** decide on suitable key words. The computer will search for **exactly** what you type in. The words you choose should be the kind of word or phrase which might occur in the title of an article or in

a descriptive summary of the article. Keep your search terms as simple as possible and avoid words like *the*, *of*, *with* or *to*. Remember that most databases are American, with American spellings.

6. **Decide on your search strategy:** before beginning, it is worth spending a few minutes working out your search strategy. Write down some possible keywords and combinations. Type in your keywords or phrases one at a time and then use the facilities of the individual database to narrow down your search.

7. **Narrow down your 'hits':** aim to have no more than 70–75 hits to look at. If you have more than 75, you need to make your search more specific. Select subdivisions to narrow them down.

8. **Record your search:** if possible, copy the results of your search onto your own computer disk. Make sure that you take a disk with you or that you know where you can buy one in the library.

9. **Look elsewhere:** once you have exhausted the resources in the library, you may still need more information. Try some of the following:

   ▩ journals not held in the library. You can obtain these from the British Library. This will take 3 to 4 weeks

   ▩ other local libraries

Tips for using the library effectively

DO

※ **Avoid queues:** find out when the library is busy and go during off-peak times. Staff are more available to help during the quiet periods.

※ **List your topics for research before you go** to the library to avoid having to make repeat visits to fill in the gaps.

※ **Ask for advice,** but first check that there is not another way of finding the information you are looking for, eg a printed pamphlet or the 'Help' section on a computer.

※ **Form learning groups** to share out the work of researching a topic. Take it in turns to go to the library to photocopy relevant material and distribute it to the members of your group.

※ **Book in advance:** make any necessary bookings, eg desk loans, CD-ROMs, before you go to the library.

DON'T

※ **Photocopy all articles.** It is a waste of money and time to photocopy articles which you do not read. Save time and money by skim reading the material quickly. Take notes as necessary and move on to the next article.

※ **Use the library to socialize** with your friends, there are many more conducive places to do this. Remember there will be times when you will be looking for somewhere quiet to work.

※ **Forget to take your library card** if you want to take out books.

5 Getting the most from lectures, seminars and tutorials

This chapter:

▧ explains the different purposes of lectures, seminars and tutorials

▧ describes what happens at them

▧ gives ideas to help you get the most from them

Why have lectures?

Lectures are the most usual form of teaching in higher education, but they do not provide you with the whole content of the subject. Their general function is to present the main ideas, and create awareness of the current debates and issues in the subject area. Lecturers try to stimulate your thinking, outline the topics for study and get you to follow up references and do further work on your own.

What to expect

There will probably be one lecture a week for each subject that you are taking. Although the lecture is generally timetabled for one hour, it usually only lasts for 55 minutes, to allow time for questions. Lectures vary in style and in the numbers of students attending. At some lectures as many as 200–300 students may be present.

Lectures are essentially a one way communication process. During a lecture you are not normally expected to participate, just sit, listen and make notes. Lectures:

▓ communicate the same information to a large number of people

▓ help you understand the ideas in the subject

▓ present some of the newest research in the field

▓ review literature that is difficult to find

▓ have a greater impact than reading a book

▓ communicate enthusiasm and attitudes

▓ organize and integrate ideas

▓ challenge your thinking on a subject, so that you end with more questions than when you started. This could be just what you need to help you get to grips with the subject, rather than just skim its surface

Generally lectures are not compulsory although it is advisable to attend, since at the very least the lecturer will provide you with an overall map of the subject. If you cannot attend, make sure that you have some way of collecting handouts and borrowing the notes of another student. You also need to keep up with the reading and preparation for tutorials or seminars.

Types of lecture

The purpose of the lecture will vary according to the subject you are studying. The lecture may be:

▓ sequential: one point developing on from the last

▓ a survey of basic ideas

▓ problem centred: the problem being stated at the beginning, various solutions discussed and evidence for and against each solution considered

▓ an overview of different perspectives on a single concept

▓ a consideration and evaluation of different views on the same issue

The structure of a lecture

Lectures are usually divided into three parts:

▓ **Introduction:** this gives a brief overview of what will be discussed. The aim of the lecture may be explained, an outline of its broad structure given or the problem which the lecture will address will be stated. There may also be a brief summary of what was covered in the preceding lectures and how that material links in.

▓ **Body:** this is where the key concepts are presented. These are usually sign-posted by repetition and explanation of the important points.

▓ **Conclusion:** in the conclusion the lecturer goes over and summarizes what has been covered in the lecture.

Styles of lecturing

Different lecturers and tutors have their own approach to their subject and their own style of teaching. Some lecturers:

▓ adopt a very thorough approach. They go through things in great detail and perhaps give you comprehensive handouts

▨ concentrate on the 'big picture' showing how their subject fits into the wide scheme of things. They leave you to fill in the detail for yourself

▨ think that the most important thing is to show you why they find their subject so interesting and exciting, and are less concerned with *'teaching'* you

▨ like students to interact with them, to ask questions and make comments during the lecture

▨ feel that too many interruptions spoil the flow of the lecture and prefer questions to be raised afterwards or in the seminars

You need to get used to the different styles of delivery so that you get maximum benefit. Whatever the style of the lecturer, getting the most from a lecture will require effort on your part.

'Good' and 'bad' lecturers

You may be lucky enough to have lecturers who are good at communicating their enthusiasm for their subject, who are able to hold your attention and are entertaining. This won't always be the case. It is helpful to remember that lecturers are in the job because they know about their subject, not because they are good entertainers and performers. If they are, then it is a bonus. However, you may find that although some lectures are immensely entertaining, you come away thinking *'What did I learn?'*.

It is worth remembering that you go to lectures to learn. The lecturer's primary aim may be to inform you rather than excite your interest in the subject matter. Even the best lecturer can sometimes seem boring.

However if, over time, you find the method of delivery is getting in the way of understanding the subject, go and speak to the lecturer concerned. Talk to the lecturer about the difficulties you are having and try to find ways that would make things easier for you. You may well find that in an informal situation the lecturer is relaxed and able to discuss the problem with you.

Preparation for lectures

To get the most from lectures, you need a reasonable grasp of the subject matter. Before you attend a lecture:

Get a syllabus for every unit you are studying

This will outline the scope of the topics to be covered in the lectures. It may also include the weeks when each topic will be covered and the recommended reading or key references that relate to them. It should also give you a guide to how the unit will be assessed. Relate the title of the lecture to the syllabus. Work out how it fits into the whole picture of the course.

Do the reading

The course syllabus should indicate what reading you are expected to do before each lecture. The lecturer may well comment on this reading in the lecture and you will be at a disadvantage if it is unfamiliar to you. If you have been given handouts or case studies in advance and you are expected to read them, the lecturer will assume you have done the basic work and deliver the lecture at a pace that reflects this. Do not expect the lecturer to stop and explain ideas that were explained in the reading.

Warm up your mind

You need to familiarize yourself with the topic before you walk into the lecture room. If you come cold to the lecture, you will have little idea of what the main concepts and important ideas are, when they are introduced and discussed. You will also be unsure of what to note down. Your warm up should only take about five minutes. As part of the warm up programme you could:

▓ scan the relevant chapters in your course text book to familiarize yourself with the main headings and help set a mental framework so you can orientate the material

▓ review your notes of the previous week's lecture. There is usually a logical sequence to the lecture programme, one topic following on from or building on another

Arrive in time

Arrive in time so that you can collect any handouts before the lecture begins and so that you can get a seat near the front. The acoustics in some lecture theatres are poor, so if you sit at the back you may have trouble hearing. Also talkative students often sit near the back and stop other people from concentrating. Sitting near the front will enable you to hear what is being said and see the white-board, the overhead projector screen and the video monitor.

Have the proper equipment

You need at least two pens, since one pen is bound to run dry at the most important point! You may like to have a highlighter or coloured pens so that you can emphasize important points. You should also bring a loose leaf pad, bound note books or a folder, whichever you prefer. You might also need some graph or plain paper, a ruler, or calculator depending on the nature of the lecture.

Don't rush off

The minute you hear the lecturer say '*... and to sum up*', don't start to pack away your things and get up. As the summary is made, you will be able to see if you have captured all the important points in your notes and identify any gaps. Directly following the lecture is also a good time to ask the lecturer for clarification on any points that you do not understand, or at least book a time when you can come and ask about them.

During the lecture

You have two main tasks during the lecture:

1. listen actively to the presentation
2. make a good set of notes to act as a permanent record of what was discussed.

These two activities are linked. Active listening is the basis of effective notemaking. If you do not listen well, you will not be able to construct a comprehensive set of notes. You need to make notes of what you hear in order to retain the information. You can't rely on your memory. Unless you make a record, you forget 50 per cent of what you hear within five minutes of hearing it. Twenty-four hours later you can remember only 20 per cent of what you heard. After three weeks, you remember only 10 per cent of what you heard.

Develop active listening skills

During the lecture you need to listen actively, so that you really understand what is being discussed, rather than just mechanically noting down what the lecturer is saying or copying the content of the overhead transparencies. Listening for most people is the most natural form of learning. It is how you learned to speak and how you gained knowledge and experience until you could read and write. Although to some extent you do learn to listen instinctively, by watching people's faces and hearing the tone of voice, learning to listen is still a skill most of us need to develop.

Learning how to listen and concentrate on what is being said will not only help you get the most from your lectures, but will also help you, for example when receiving complicated instructions or working in a group.

Active listening is difficult

Active listening requires you to shut off your own thoughts and focus your full attention on what the other person is saying. A number of things, however, get in the way of doing this:

It is hard to concentrate
You can listen and think four times faster than you can speak. The average person talks at about 125 words per minute, but you can think at speeds of up to 500 words a minute. People often use the surplus time that is available to let their minds wander off on a different track and so stop listening to what is being said.

You get distracted
While you are trying to concentrate on what someone is saying, other unwanted messages keep intruding. You may have internal distractions, for example: a headache, feel tired from lack of sleep or have hunger pains. You may be distracted by external factors: it may be too hot in the room; too stuffy; you might hear noises from outside; people may be arriving late and creating a disturbance.

You get bored
If you are not interested in a subject, you may become more interested in your own thoughts. You mentally 'switch off' from boredom or thinking you know the subject already. Be prepared to fight this!

You may not like the person who is talking or what is being discussed
This can mean you sometimes completely block out what is being said and just spend your time reacting to it.

You misinterpret what someone is saying
You can never be sure that what you hear is what the speaker said or indeed meant. Particular words mean different things to different people, so you may be on a completely different track to that of the speaker.

You don't understand a point or concept and then you switch off. By switching off, you won't be able to understand or follow the rest of what is being said.

Effective listening requires you to shut off from any distraction and really concentrate on what is being said. It is an active, not a passive process and is one of the basic requirements for listening to lectures.

How to be an active listener

▓ *Pick out the main details from the less important ones: 'there are four main reasons for ...'.*

▓ *Understand what is being said, rephrase the points in your head, 'so what that means is ...'.*

▓ *Mentally summarize what has been said so far.*

▓ *Make notes to aid your concentration and help you remember what was said.*

▓ *Think of examples that support what is being said.*

▓ *Ask yourself if you agree with what is being said.*

▓ *Listen even if you don't agree, write your disagreements in the margin to consider later.*

▓ *Keep your prejudices to a minimum: ignore what the person is wearing, irritating mannerisms or poor presentation.*

▓ *Watch for body language and the pitch and pace of the speaker's voice: words that are emphasized; a slowing down to indicate the importance of a point; gestures; facial expressions. Over 50 per cent of the message is unspoken.*

Put simply, active listening requires you to:

Stop! *concentrating on yourself and your feelings about the lecturer.*

Look! *for non verbal clues: the overhead projector slides, what's written on the white-board, gestures, facial expression.*

Listen! *for verbal signs that help you work out the structure of the lecture: slight breaks, tone of voice or specific phrases such as 'moving on …', 'arguments against this are …', 'at the centre of the debate are …', points being repeated, saying things more loudly or more slowly.*

Problems with lectures

If you can't concentrate:

▓ **Challenge your mind.** Ask yourself questions. Any question is likely to improve your concentration. Some questions you could ask yourself might be: where is the lecture going? What is the relationship between the present topic and the previous ones? What are the three most examinable points in the lecture?

▓ **Change the position in which you are sitting.** You may have become too comfortable.

You may need to make a real effort to concentrate on what is being said, but if you don't you will have wasted your time in attending.

When you get distracted:
- **Ignore irritating mannerisms.** Lecturers can be quite distracting if they have particular mannerisms that irritate you. Try to ignore these. Counting how many times someone says *'um'* or *'you know'* is really not a very productive way of using your time.

- **Move away from disruptive students.** Other students can be a source of distraction. It may be useful to move away from students who chatter. Sitting nearer the front will also reduce the number of people in your field of vision.

When you can't keep up with the lecturer:
- **If you are getting left behind noting down only the major points,** leave a gap and then add the missing material after the lecture.

- **Do your preparation.** You may recognize graphs, charts or other material that the lecturer is using. All you then need to do is note the title of the graph or chart in the margin of your notes and, using your textbook, add it after the lecture.

- **Discuss the problem with other students** and consider seeing the lecturer as a group and suggesting a slightly slower pace.

If you can't follow what is being said:
- **Make a list of points that you do not understand** and ask the lecturer about them afterwards.

- **Do the required reading** so that you are familiar with the ideas being discussed. The lecturer may just be highlighting the most important points and assuming that you have completed the pre-reading.

Recording your lectures

It may seem an attractive idea to make a cassette recording of your lectures to ensure that you do not miss out on any of the important points. There are, however, disadvantages to recording your lectures:

▓ you may not concentrate in the lecture

▓ you need to find time to play through the recording and make notes

▓ you need to get permission from the lecturer

Seminars and tutorials

What are they?

Seminars and tutorials are a form of group work. They offer you the opportunity of meeting regularly with a tutor to discuss topics related to the subject you are studying. Seminar groups are larger than tutorial groups and the exact size of groups varies between different institutions. At some institutions there might, for example, be 20 students in a seminar group and 10 in a tutorial.

Why have them?

Seminars and tutorials are designed to deepen your understanding, by working actively with others on topics related to your subject. They also bring you into relatively close contact with a member of staff.

Working with others in this way, you can integrate what you have learned from lectures and reading by:

▓ questioning information

▓ clarifying your own thoughts

▓ evaluating the views of others as well as your own

▓ defending your point of view in a calm and logical manner

▓ developing a different view point

▓ arriving at new conclusions

In addition you can:

▓ practise communicating ideas to others

▓ practise your verbal skills in a semi-formal setting

▓ develop your ability to listen

▓ increase your self confidence

▓ develop your interpersonal skills

▓ be motivated to do further study

As you can see from the above, it is very important to attend all your seminars and tutorials. But you need to do more than just attend, to get the maximum benefit.

Preparation

Do any required preparation. Part of this will probably involve reading. If you don't do the reading, you won't have anything useful to contribute to the discussion. If you prepare you will have a clearer idea of what you want to say and you will remember the discussion more clearly.

As you do the reading, write out any questions that you have or ideas that you could contribute to the discussion. If everyone in the group does the preparation, the discussion has the necessary ingredients for success.

What happens at tutorials and seminars?

Tutorials and seminars are your chance to speak up about your interests in the subject and give your opinions. They should be an interactive exchange of information and ideas. Their success depends on you. It is not the tutor's responsibility to ensure that all goes well; it is a team effort. You are expected to:

Contribute to the discussion

Don't wait until you have something really important to say before speaking up. Just saying that you don't understand is a useful contribution, because other people will be worrying about the same thing.

If you are nervous about speaking, build up your self confidence by careful preparation. This should help you to contribute to the discussion, as you will already have developed some ideas about the topic. Get to know the other students, so that they are no longer strangers, but a group of friends and colleagues. By talking to other members of the group, you will see that you are by no means the only one having trouble with a particular point.

Don't feel self critical if you say very little in some discussions. Some people are just more talkative in groups than others and you may find it difficult to get a word in! You can still learn by listening closely.

Ask questions

Some people worry about asking questions in a group. They think their question might be thought silly, or they do not like to interrupt. Remember that questions are a useful way to straighten out a difficult issue. If you are puzzled, chances are other people are having the same problems. Questions can let the tutor know that there is a gap in understanding in the group. The tutor then has a chance to explain in more detail.

Give papers

Sometimes you may be asked to prepare a 'paper' to deliver to the group. This involves presenting your own ideas about a subject and leading a discussion. You need to prepare very thoroughly for this (see Chapters 10 and 12). Presenting a paper is one of the best ways of learning about a subject. Having to explain your point of view to someone else is a good way to see whether you really understand it.

Taking notes

During a seminar or tutorial, it is more important to listen and contribute than write everything down. It is also difficult to take notes when there is a large degree of participation. You only need to note down the main points of the discussion, the key ideas. Mind maps (see Chapter 6) are very useful for this kind of note making because they allow you to note down apparently unrelated points.

How to make the most of tutorials and seminars

▧ Arrange times to meet with other students outside appointed tutorial times. You can get a lot from group study and informal discussion. It also helps to consolidate your groups and make people feel more comfortable about talking in tutorials.

▧ Don't let your group sessions degenerate into monologues by the tutor. You should have as much discussion with other students as with the lecturer. Indeed, the debate should be able to continue even if the tutor is absent. Most tutors welcome discussion and try to stimulate it, but their efforts are not always successful. If tutors start out by asking questions and there is no response, it is likely that the session will become a mini lecture. Do the preparation, so that you have something to discuss.

If the group is not working well, openly discuss the reasons for this.

After the tutorial spend a few minutes going over what was discussed and what was concluded.

Lectures, seminars and tutorials: key points

Do your preparation.

Participate by listening actively and contributing to discussions.

Develop strategies to cope with any problems.

6 Making notes

This chapter:

▨ emphasizes the importance of note making as an active study skill

▨ explains two different styles of note making

▨ describes how to supplement your notes

Why are good notes important?

You will spend a significant amount of your study time in situations where note making is required, for example attending lectures, seminars, tutorials and reading. Without notes you will quickly forget the main points that you have read or heard. Also note making requires you to be actively involved in the studying process.

Note making

Note **making** is an active task and should not be confused with note **taking** which is passive and implies that you are simply writing down what you hear without filtering it. Note making is an intellectual activity. To make good notes you need to select, analyse and summarize what you hear. You also need to be able to strike a balance between listening actively to what is being said and making a record of it.

Effective note making is an active way of studying as it can:

▨ force you to think, because you have to make decisions about what to write down

▨ help you pay attention to what you are listening to, or reading

▨ aid your understanding of new material if the notes are in your own words and organized in your own way

▨ help you realize when you don't understand what is being said

▨ aid concentration

▨ act as a memory aid. You remember things better if you have written them down. You will have forgotten about 80 per cent of what was said in 24 hours

▨ make it easier to distinguish between important points and detail

▨ provide a permanent record

▨ facilitate learning. Some lectures cannot be fully understood during the lecture itself but become clear later when you review your notes

Styles of note making

This section offers you some ideas about two different styles of note making you could adopt. Whichever style of note making you decide to use, you need to aim to put a structure on your material. The method you choose depends on the purpose the notes will serve. There is no one perfect system. All that is important, is that the system works for you.

Linear key concept notes

The aim in this style of note making is to record the basic points in a way that will trigger your memory when you come to review them. During a lecture, it is not enough simply to condense what is being said and copy down the overhead transparencies. To make good key concept notes, you need to understand the lecture or what you are reading and be making decisions about what to note down and how to summarize points.

How to make key concept notes

▓ Divide your notes into numbered sections with:

    clear headings

    underlinings

    subdivisions

    indentations.

▓ To help you organize the material you could divide your page into two or three columns by folding the paper lengthways. You then use:

    the left hand column for main headings

    the centre column for sub headings and details

    the right hand column for your own comments.

▓ Record key ideas.

▓ Summarize important points.

▓ Condense difficult points.

▓ Note down words and phrases, not complete sentences. These take too long to write and too long to read when reviewing your notes.

▓ Use diagrams, tables, charts, boxes, arrows and brackets; anything that will help put a structure on what you have written.

Remember:

▓ In lectures, seminars and tutorials, note the session's topic, the tutor's name and the date on the first page of your notes. This will help you spot any gaps and make it easier to retrieve a particular set of notes.

▓ When reading, note all the reference details. (See Chapter 8 for further ideas about making notes of your reading.)

▓ Number your pages in case they get out of order.

▓ Leave plenty of space on each page so that you can add points later.

▓ Organize your notes; number or letter the sections.

▓ Make your own notes in the margins, for example: *know for exams*, *good essay question topic*, *unclear*.

▓ Note key words like: *examinable*, *assessable*, *must know* and any other term that suggests the concept being discussed is important and likely to appear on an examination paper.

▓ Note down the names of major writers and the dates of their work.

▓ Note any references to course texts and handouts.

▓ Make a note if you are referred back to a previous topic, or forward to something not yet covered.

▓ Note diagrams and charts.

▓ Consider taking your textbook to class with you, to use as a reference.

▓ Use different coloured pens for emphasis.

Abbreviations and symbols to aid note making

If you use a range of symbols and abbreviations, you can make notes more efficiently. Appendix C gives a sample glossary of the kind of abbreviations you can use to speed up your own note making.

Advantages of linear key concept notes

▨ Listening becomes an active process where you wait to hear something significant before you note it down.

▨ You are following the sense of what is being said.

▨ You have more energy for observing the pattern and structure of what is being said, and don't get lost in the detail.

▨ You have a neat set of notes for revision that can be quickly scanned for significant points.

▨ The key ideas serve as a stimulus for reviving your memory.

▨ They help with creative thinking which centres on ideas and concepts, not on detail.

Mind maps or pattern notes

Mind map notes are a way of building up an entire picture on a single theme or topic by using key words which describe whole ideas (Buzan with Buzan, 1993). They are called mind maps because they are an attempt to make notes in a similar way to how the mind works. Linear notes use only the left side of the brain. Mind maps use both sides of the brain and also reflect the brain's natural way of processing information in an interlinked and integrated way.

Mind maps (see Figure 2) begin with a central idea from which ideas branch outwards. Ideas can be fitted in whenever they occur and connections between the branches can easily be made. They use keywords and trigger words. You can also use simple drawings.

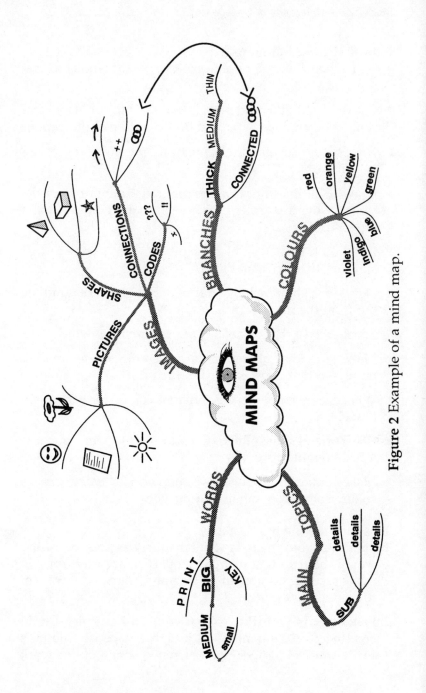

Figure 2 Example of a mind map.

How to draw mind maps

▓ Turn a blank sheet of unlined A4 paper (or larger) so that it is wider than it is long.

▓ Use coloured pens and pencils (not just blue or black) and write the name of the subject in the middle of the paper.

▓ If possible, surround the name by a drawing that symbolizes the subject.

▓ Draw thick lines or *main branches* radiating out from the central word and drawing. These lines represent the main aspects of the subject.

▓ Label each branch in block capitals, with a *keyword* that sums up that particular idea.

▓ Develop each branch by adding thinner lines that radiate out from the main branch.

▓ Label each of these *smaller branches* with a keyword.

▓ Make sure that all branches are connected to another branch so that there is a clear structure.

▓ Whenever possible, use a different colour for each main branch.

▓ Use drawings and illustrations to help trigger your creative thought processes.

▓ Make connections between the branches by using arrows, colours, shapes, symbols and images.

Tips for drawing mind maps

1. **Put down your ideas as spontaneously as possible**, don't worry about sorting them into a particular order. You can do a second version of your mind map as a way of reviewing your notes

2. **Pick colours you like**, so that you can have pleasure in creating the mind map. Although choice of colour is really a matter of personal preference, some colours work

better than others, for example strong colours for the main branches.

3. **Add drawings when you review the notes**. Drawings are not there to make the mind map look pretty! They are an important part of mind mapping because you have to select visual images that capture the ideas. Also, while you are drawing, you are spending more time thinking about the idea.

4. **Add two or three quotations** when making a mind map from a chapter of a book.

Advantages of mind maps

▓ Each pattern has a unique shape which makes it easier to recall.

▓ Your visual memory is better than your verbal one, so this makes pattern notes easier to recall than other notes.

▓ You can see the relative importance of an idea. The closer it is to the centre, the more important it is.

▓ They are flexible. New information can easily be added without the need to squeeze it in.

▓ Links between ideas are easy to see.

▓ They are fun because they are colourful, creative and enjoyable to construct!

If you are new to mind mapping, it may take you a little time to get used to working with them. You may prefer to practise first on making mind map notes as a way of refining a set of linear key concept notes, rather than start by using them to make your lecture notes. Mind maps are particularly useful when making summary notes as part of your exam preparation (see Chapter 13).

Developing your own style

There is no single best way of taking notes. Note making is a very personal process. You may discover that you develop techniques that are very different from the linear key concept and mind map notes mentioned above. Devise a system that suits your needs. Learn from the useful features of other students' notes and ideas in general about how to make good notes.

Whatever style you develop, your notes need to show:

▓ the lecture's structure

▓ the main points

▓ subpoints

▓ supporting details

Share the work of note making in lectures with another student
One of you can concentrate on taking notes as fully as possible, while the other one concentrates on following the tutor's train of thought. Afterwards you can get together to produce a joint record of the lecture.

How much do you need to write?

There are three levels of note making:

1. Very comprehensive
This kind of note making involves writing down as much of what is said as is possible. The system does have disadvantages:

▓ Few of us can write at a speed that is fast enough for us to write down every word a person says, which could be 150 words a minute.

▓ Even if you could write quickly enough, you would focus all your attention and energy on note making rather than listening.

▓ Too many notes can be almost as big a problem as not enough. You will need to work through them later to condense them down and pull out the main ideas and concepts.

You need to be selective in what you write. Most tutors usually rely on repetition to emphasize a point. You don't need to do this so much when you are writing. Trying to take down everything can sometimes be a safety measure for people who do not understand the material. They take down everything since they cannot distinguish the important from the unimportant.

You may sometimes need to make very comprehensive notes if you are unable to follow the lecture. But, because of its disadvantages, this system should only be used in emergencies.

2. Key concept notes
This is the most useful system of note making. It requires you to be selective about what you write, while capturing the basic structure and ideas in the lecture. Linear key concept notes and mind mapping are ways of key concept note making.

3. Skeleton notes or none at all
If the lecture is designed to stimulate your imagination or is about a philosophical concept, you may find you spend most of your time listening and take only the briefest notes. Remember however, notes about ideas are as important as those about information. After all, you made the effort to attend the lecture in the first place and unless you take some notes, you will remember only a small part of what was discussed. Mind mapping might be the most useful method of note making in this context.

Finishing your notes

Review and finish off your notes while you can still remember them and can interpret what you wrote. Aim to do this on the day of the lecture. A single word may be enough to remind you of an example at the time of making the notes, but a week later you may have forgotten what the shorthand means. The review process requires you to think. Don't simply go through your notes underlining or highlighting points.

When reviewing your notes:

▓ check you can read what you have written

▓ check that you have an accurate record of what was covered

▓ make sure you understand the main points and how they relate to each other

▓ ensure that the structure of the lecture is clear

▓ make sure that you file any relevant articles or handouts with your notes.

Then:

▓ Work through your notes to make a list of all the things that you don't understand and then use this list as the basis for asking questions of your tutor, fellow students or anyone else who may be able to answer them for you.

▓ Make summaries of your notes, then make a summary of the summaries.

▓ Draw a mind map or write a single paragraph summary of the main points of the lecture.

▓ Write key concepts or ideas on index cards.

▓ Make a list of all the things that aren't clear to you. Cross them off the list as you come to understand them.

❋ Go through your notes and try to think of anything that contradicts what you have written.

❋ For every example in your notes, try to think of a counter example.

Supplement your notes
Once you have completed this first review of your notes, you need to supplement them with reading and your own thoughts and comments. To supplement your lecture notes:

❋ Make additional notes in seminars.

❋ Ask for clarification of points that you did not understand in the lecture. Note down the tutor's answer with examples.

❋ Work through any handouts you have been given. Don't just file them away without a glance. Work through them to check that you understand the material they contain. Note any questions that you have and ask them in your next tutorial.

❋ Add additional notes you make when you are reading books and articles.

Organizing your notes

Having taken trouble to make the notes in the first place, it is easy to end up with a pile of notes that are so disorganized that you cannot face trying to find out what you want. You need to organize a storage system for them.

Keep the storage system simple. For example, use loose leaf binders with perhaps one which you take along to class for all that day's notes and a number at home for each separate subject, divided into separate themes. At the end of the day or week, transfer your notes from the day file into the subject file. Check all your notes have headings, are dated and have the source noted.

Learn your notes

These notes will be your major resource when preparing for exams. Each week, spend a few hours going through your lecture notes and learn them as if you were going to be examined in them. Periodic learning is much better than trying to cram everything in at the last minute.

Making notes: key points

▓ Use a style of note making that is appropriate to the activity.

▓ Be selective in what you write.

▓ Work through your lecture notes on the same day, clarifying points where necessary.

Reference

Buzan, T. with Buzan, B., *The Mind Map Book*, London, BBC Books, 1993.

7 Developing your reading skills

This chapter:

▓ explains how to use seven different reading techniques

▓ considers effective rather than faster reading

▓ takes you through the three stages of reading

Why read about reading?

You are expected to undertake a considerable quantity and variety of reading as part of your study programme. To enable you to make the most efficient use of your reading time, you need a variety of reading approaches. The following chapter describes a number of different approaches to reading. It also looks at the skills needed and the most appropriate uses for each reading technique.

Different types of reading

Once you have learnt to read, reading can become a skill which you take for granted. You develop, probably unconsciously, a set of reading techniques that enable you to tackle most of the usual kinds of reading materials. When reading novels you sit absorbed for hours, when reading magazines you read in short bursts and when reading newspapers you read some articles closely and only glance at others.

To be successful in your studies, you need a number of reading techniques to achieve different purposes. To cope with all the demands of academic texts, you need to be able to select the most appropriate technique for the task. You also need to be able to control the intensity and speed with which you examine a text according to your needs and the time available. To be able to do all of this, you may need to extend your existing repertoire of reading skills.

Figure 3 details a number of different approaches to reading. As you can see, what you want to get from reading, your purpose, determines the reading technique that you should use.

Academic materials are usually presented differently from discipline to discipline and the way in which you are supposed to read them also varies. Therefore, before you start reading, ask yourself, *'How should I read this particular piece?'*. Since different purposes for reading need different reading techniques, you need to select your reading method with both your purpose and the nature of the reading material in mind.

Whatever kind of reading technique you use, you need to read actively as opposed to passively. A passive reader looks at and recognizes the words on a page, but doesn't actively engage with the material. If you sit looking at the printed text and your mind is elsewhere or you cannot recall or explain or ask questions about what you have read, then you are reading passively. Making notes will help you be more active in your reading. (See Chapter 8 for further details of note making and reading.)

Reading techniques: what is involved?

Scan reading

Scan reading is a very useful skill which enables you quickly to get a general idea of the topic or to find specific facts. **Scan reading is useful when you want to:**

What you want to achieve	Reading technique	What is involved
locate specific information	scan	searching the text looking for key words and phrases
gain a general overview	skim	rapid reading to understand the general meaning
develop full understanding, get detailed information	in depth	careful, slow and repetitive reading that requires a high level of concentration
read for background	extensive	reading large amounts in a single session
assess and evaluate information and ideas	critical	questioning and analysing to determine the author's purpose
revision	rapid	confirming knowledge
proof reading	intensive	thorough reading, checking spelling, punctuation and sentence structure, requires a high level of concentration

Figure 3 Different reading techniques.

▓ locate specific information

▓ find out whether a book might be useful to you

▓ decide whether to read a text in detail

▓ add to your store of information on a subject that is familiar to you

Scanning is a preliminary process, a first look at a text. It is the kind of reading you do when looking at a book or journal to see if you can locate the information that you need. It is not designed to give you a thorough understanding of what you are reading. Instead it helps you find your way around the material.

Techniques for scanning

▓ **Use the table of contents, the index, chapter headings and subheadings** to guide you to the item or section that you want (see Figure 4).

▓ **Run your eyes down each page and take note of any terms in bold print** or in italics, section headings, graphs, charts or anything else which seems to jump out at you.

▓ **Be alert and active** since you need to register and analyse what you see, noting the main themes or points and forming an overall impression of what you read.

▓ Be prepared to jump backwards and forwards in the text as you search for information.

▓ Make a note of the terms picked up by scanning. Only write the term, not a definition. The act of writing will help record the information in your memory. Having noted several terms and concepts during the scanning process, your mind will be alert for them when they occur during more intense reading.

Title/subtitle: a brief guide to the book's contents. This is rarely able to show the scope of the book.

Author: the name and possibly information to show how qualified the writer is in this field.

Publication details: including when the book was written, if it has been reprinted or revised, the publication date of your copy.

Contents: the framework of the book.

Preface/foreword/introduction: this may have information about why the book was written. Since the introduction is the last thing to be written, it may give a guide to the author's latest thinking about the subject.

Text: the opening and closing paragraphs of each chapter may act as a summary to the whole chapter.

Conclusion: if the book has a conclusion, it is a good idea to read this first as it probably outlines the direction of the author's thinking throughout the book.

Glossary: a list of the technical words and jargon used in the book.

Bibliography/references: a list of the writer's sources.

Appendix: a supplement, usually at the end of the book, containing extra information such as statistical charts.

Figure 4 How a book is organized.

Skim reading

Skim reading is a basic academic skill. It involves reading quickly through a text to understand the general meaning and to gain a grasp of the kind of problems and issues in the text. You might find skim reading a little difficult if it is new to you, but it is well worth putting time and effort into perfecting this useful technique.

Skim reading is useful when:

▨ reading supplementary materials such as reports, articles in journals, newspaper accounts

▨ looking for a few key facts which you do not need to read in depth

▨ you are trying to decide if a text is worth more detailed study

Techniques for skim reading

▨ **Look for key sentences.** These will generally be the first, second or perhaps even the last sentence in the paragraph. Reading the key sentences helps you gain an understanding of the structure of the work and form ideas about what is important in it.

▨ **Read the introductory and concluding paragraphs** of each chapter. The introduction will give you an overview and the final paragraphs generally provide a summary.

▨ **Look at the organization and structure of the text** to get a general feel of what it is about. Information tends to be concentrated at the beginning and end of written material. Summary results and conclusions should always be read first as they contain the essence of the material.

▨ **Check the last chapter**, it is sometimes a complete summary of the book.

▨ **Set yourself questions** to provide focus for your reading.

The following are examples of questions you could use:

What is the book about?

When was it written?

Who is the author?

Why did the author write the book?

What is the general approach and line of argument?

What style and layout are used?

▓ **Vary your reading speed.** Slow down over some key passages and read quickly over others.

▓ **Be prepared to return to the material at a later time** in order to understand fully what is in the text.

▓ **Make outline notes** of the main points (see Chapter 8).

In depth reading

This is the kind of reading you need to do when reading about key concepts in your field of study and when you need to gain full understanding of all the details and ideas involved. It involves careful, slow and repeated reading of the text.

In depth reading helps you to:
▓ gain a complete understanding of the information and content

▓ retain information for longer than with scanning or skimming

Techniques for in depth reading
▓ Skim the material first.

▓ **Read the author's preface, study the table of contents and the index.**

▨ **Read the chapter summaries** and skim your way rapidly through the book. If you are studying a journal article, read the abstract (a summary of the whole piece).

▨ **Read the material, section by section, in detail.** Expect to read the piece more than once.

▨ **Check that you understand:**

the main argument

the information supporting it

the theoretical perspective

the underlying assumptions

▨ **Make sure that you can pick out the main ideas expressed in each paragraph.** In core texts, you will find that many authors begin a paragraph by first setting out the main idea. They then expand on it, produce supporting evidence and end with a summary sentence. If you are in any doubt about the main points the author is trying to make, concentrate on the summary first, filling in the details later.

▨ **Be prepared to refer to previous paragraphs or pages** in order to grasp the sequence of an argument.

▨ **Note down the main ideas** included in each paragraph.

Critical reading

Like in depth reading, critical reading involves gaining a complete understanding of what has been written. In addition, it involves judging the ideas put forward, the way they have been presented and also how the author's ideas fit with other writers in the same field. Critical reading therefore takes time and requires a high level of concentration.

Critical reading enables you to:
▓ determine the strengths and weaknesses of an argument

▓ assess where the author's ideas fit in the range of perspectives taken on a subject

Techniques for critical reading
(Some of these are the same as for in depth reading)

▓ **Criticize and evaluate the ideas** that you read. Agree or disagree, question evidence, dwell on particular points, contrast or link them with other points.

▓ **Check that you understand the main argument**, the information supporting it, the theoretical perspective and the underlying assumptions.

▓ **Be prepared to refer to previous paragraphs or pages** in order to grasp the sequence of an argument.

▓ **Note down the main structure of the argument.** Note also areas where you disagree with what you have read.

▓ **Work out how the ideas are expressed and how they are organized.** Critique the author's writing style and method of presentation.

▓ **Work out the author's intended message** and evaluate how effectively this message is supported by the information given.

▓ **Analyse and criticize the material to uncover how the message has been affected by the author's purpose**, biases, experience and beliefs.

▓ **Relate what you are reading to what else has been written** on the subject. Assess how it fits with what you already know.

Rapid reading

Rapid reading is, in some ways, similar to skim reading. It enables you to progress quickly through a text because you do not read every word, sentence or paragraph. Unlike skim reading, however, with rapid reading you make fast progress, not as a result of the techniques you use, but because you are already familiar with the material. What you are doing is half reading and half filling in the gaps from memory.

Rapid reading is useful for:
▓ rereading already familiar material

▓ revision

Intensive reading

This involves careful, slow reading, making sure that you check and understand every word, as you would do if you were signing a contract.

Use intensive reading to:
▓ proof read your own and others' written work

Techniques for intensive reading
▓ **Read the material section by section** in detail.

▓ **Check spelling, punctuation and sentence length.**

▓ **Review the structure.** Check that the paragraphing is appropriate.

▓ **Insert key sentences, introductions and conclusions** if they are missing.

Extensive reading

Although somewhat similar to skim reading, extensive reading is a more thorough method of reading. When reading extensively you read everything, but do not necessarily pause to reflect. This enables you to read large amounts in a single session.

Extensive reading is useful for:
* reading for background information
* reading for pleasure, eg a novel

Effective versus faster reading

When faced with a situation which requires reading more material than ever before, it is understandable to worry about your ability to cope. Learning to speed read is not, however, the solution to the problem of large amounts of reading. Aiming to read **effectively**, rather than more quickly, is a much better approach.

Being a *fast* or *slow* reader has little to do with the effectiveness of your reading. Everybody reads at different speeds according to:

* the difficulty of the text
* their purpose in reading
* the reading techniques they are using
* how tired they are
* how interested they are
* their environment.

If you think your reading speed is slower than some other students, remember that understanding and recall of the material are not related to speed. Efficient reading is not so much concerned with the time you take to read, but with the **usefulness** of the work that you have done.

Rather than trying to learn to speed read, you are better off using the full range of different reading techniques available. As you become more familiar with the language and content of what you read, your reading speed will automatically increase.

To read more effectively:

- **Vary your reading speed** according to your purpose. Textbooks usually need to be read much more slowly and perhaps reread several times before they are fully understood. A single paragraph or diagram in a textbook may have to be read through slowly four or five times. Pages that are worth studying should be read as slowly as possible and reread until they are understood.

- **Divide up your reading sessions.** Your span of concentration is limited so plan a number of sessions each week, rather than attempting one long session.

- **Skim read all material before you read it.** This may take time at the start of your reading session, however it will enable you to decide which parts of the material are important for your purpose. You can then vary your reading rate, according to the importance of the information and ideas.

The three stages of reading

1. preparation

2. reading

3. reflection, rereading and revision

Stage 1: preparation

Determine your purpose
Before you begin to read, clarify your purpose. Then ask yourself: 'How should I read this piece?'. Remember that you need to approach the material differently depending on your purpose. Although you may be reading the same text,

when you read for background, your approach will be different from when you are reading it as a core text. Before you begin reading, check through Figure 3 (Different reading techniques) to help you select the most appropriate technique.

Set your reading goals
Setting reading goals gives focus and provides a way of assessing the effectiveness of your reading session. When you are reading for an assessment, you already have a goal. If you are having trouble setting a goal, it can be useful to look at old assessments and examination papers. They provide a useful source of ideas and problems on which to focus.

Decide on the time for this reading session
There is a limited amount that you can take in from reading in a single sitting. This limit depends on how complex the material is, how familiar you are with the subject, how well it is presented and your own level of concentration. Allow time between reading sessions to think about and reflect on what you read.

Decide how much material to cover
Determine how many pages it is realistic to cover in the time available. You might like to mark the beginning and end of your target section. In this way you will have a measure of the progress you make.

Set yourself questions to answer during your reading
Doing this helps you because it gives your reading a purpose. Having a questioning attitude will also help you read books critically. Your questions provide a framework into which you can fit what you read. If the subject is unfamiliar to you, skim the text before setting your questions. See below for examples of questions you might set yourself.

Stage 2: reading

Systematically scan the material
This is one of the first steps you take to become thoroughly familiar with material. It helps you get a good idea of what the text contains. As you scan, write down any ideas, questions or statements which seem relevant to your reading purpose and that might help you understand and critique the text. As mentioned earlier, you need different reading strategies to match your different reading tasks. If you only aim to scan read, then that is all that is needed in this session.

Take a more thorough approach if appropriate
If your aim is to read critically or in depth, this will take time. Using the techniques previously described, keep in mind your own purpose in study, the syllabus you are trying to cover and the relevance of the text to your own special interests.

Read actively
Work through the questions that you set yourself. Avoid questions that simply relate to factual content and comprehension. For example:

* *Does this agree with what I already know?*

* *Is this a suitable procedure?*

* *What evidence has the author for this statement?*

* *Has the author selected facts in order to build up a case?*

* *Can the facts be interpreted in another way?*

* *Is what is being said consistent with what you already know and believe?*

* *How can you apply in practice the facts, ideas and theories you have learnt?*

In addition set questions that relate to your goals.

Study tables and graphs

Complex arguments and masses of information can often be presented briefly and more clearly in a table or graph. If you skip the graphs or tables you will often miss the major points the author is trying to make. Graphs and diagrams are also much more easily remembered than the written text.

Stage 3: reflection, rereading and revision

A period of reflection is needed before you are able to say that you fully understand the ideas and concepts in a text. You need time to link what you have read with what you already know and with other ideas in the same field. As part of your reflection, you may need to return to the text to re-read it. You may need to read another account of the same subject. Each reading should increase your understanding and aid insight.

Material that has to be retained over long periods should be studied and restudied. Revision should not be regarded as only something to be undertaken just before examinations. The first revision of the material should take place soon after the original reading. You may need to make further revisions before the final revision for examinations.

Developing your reading skills: key points

▮ Determine your purpose for reading before you start.

▮ Select the reading technique that suits your purpose.

▮ Aim to read more effectively rather than to increase your reading speed.

---

8 Working with academic texts

This chapter:

▨ gives you advice about reading lists and buying books

▨ explains how to work with academic texts

Reading lists

When you begin a new subject, you will be given a reading list, which details the titles of books and articles that relate to the subject area. You are not usually expected to read all the titles on the reading list. During lectures, seminars and tutorials your tutors will refer to texts on the reading list which are relevant to particular topics. You also need to read texts on the list to:

▨ gain understanding of the subject

▨ prepare for lectures, eg by reading certain chapters from a specified text

▨ prepare for seminars and assessments, eg by reading articles, texts, and case studies

The texts referred to on the reading list are usually available in the library.

Before you buy a book or begin your reading, you need to check that you have the most up-to-date reading list.

Reading lists are usually compiled 6 months or more before a course starts. Find out from your tutors if any alterations have been made to the reading list since it was compiled. Most reading lists have a recommended book which is usually referred to as the *core* text. Check that the core text on your copy of the reading list is the one that will be used for your course. Since the list was compiled, a more recent edition may have been published or another text may have been selected.

Core texts

You need to **buy** the core text for each of the subjects you are studying. Even though there may be several reference copies of it in the library, you should not rely on being able to get hold of one of them when you need it. There may be 200 or more students on your particular course. All of them need to consult the same core text, at the same stage of the programme. If you do not have your own copy of the core text, you may find yourself waiting for two to three hours in the library to get access to a particularly popular or essential text. If demand is great, you may even find it impossible to borrow the text at all.

Buying books

Many books are expensive, so you need to be sure that you are buying the right ones. Limit your first purchases to core texts. If you find the recommended core text too difficult, ask students in the year above to give you details of the books they found useful when studying the course.

Once you have bought the core texts, you can build up a collection of additional material as seems appropriate and as your budget allows. You may decide to buy:

▓ books that you want to highlight and make notes on, and keep for future reference

▓ books on subjects that you are particularly interested in

▓ texts that are also used on other parts of your course

▓ photocopies of articles (subject to copyright laws)

Working with academic texts

You may experience difficulties when reading some of the texts on your reading list for the first time. There may be a number of reasons for this:

▓ You may be put off by the words used which may be new or unfamiliar.

▓ You may not like the author's writing style.

▓ The text is usually an argument that requires you to pay careful attention and to stop and think.

▓ Writers aim to say exactly what they mean, even if it takes a lot of extra words.

▓ Writers tend to use long, complicated sentences which can make it hard to understand the text on first reading.

▓ Academic writers are usually concerned with broad abstract questions, which they state in very cautious language.

1. Build a framework for the subject

Your progress in a new subject will usually be slow. It takes time to understand the material fully because what you are doing is beginning to build a framework of knowledge about it.

When you begin reading, you may find that you have difficulty in following the argument. This may be because you don't yet have the required background knowledge and so you are unfamiliar with the concepts used. You may find that you need to refer back to earlier pages for clarification of points that you previously read. To build up and develop a full understanding of the theoretical perspectives or key concepts on which the material is based, you may need to read other material which deals with the same subject. This is a necessary part of developing your understanding of the subject.

Sometimes, however, your slow progress may not be because you are building your understanding of the subject. What you are reading may simply be badly written. You may also be experiencing difficulties because the material is badly organized and presented.

2. Read for overview

You may find the specialist language of the subject discipline difficult to understand. If this is the case read the passage through carefully first, not worrying too much about individual words or phrases that you can't understand. A first reading like this should give you a general idea of what the passage is about and what points are being made. You can then go back to areas where you had difficulty, take each in turn and try to work out the meaning in the light of your understanding of the main ideas contained in the passage. In this way you gain an overall impression of what is written without needing to identify every word.

3. Develop your vocabulary

Make use of dictionaries. You can actively work at improving your vocabulary by using a:

▓ general dictionary
▓ technical dictionary or glossary
▓ subject dictionary

As well as a general dictionary, you may need a technical dictionary as some of the words you come across may not normally appear in a standard English dictionary. You may also find it useful to get a glossary of the technical terms used in your fields of study. Technical dictionaries often expand on a definition by giving a concrete example, which can be useful in furthering your understanding. Remember to refer back to what you were reading to see that the definition and example make sense in the context of the original text.

Develop a system for recording new words. Use a notebook or card system to write down any unfamiliar term, the context in which it appeared and its dictionary definition. If you are using a card index, write each new word on a small card and file the cards alphabetically. Practise using these new words when you write and speak.

4. Develop an analytical approach

To evaluate a piece of academic writing you need to:

▩ determine the author's purpose

▩ decide whether the text achieves its purpose

▩ compare it with other works on that subject

▩ assess how this approach differs from other writers on the same subject

▩ evaluate it against the other writers

(See *critical reading techniques* in Chapter 7.)

5. Make notes

When reading, notes help you to:

▓ remember what you read

▓ see the structure

▓ concentrate and understand

They also provide a permanent record of your reading that you can refer back to, at any time.

Making notes in your own books

Working with your own copies of texts, by highlighting or writing on them, is a good method of note making to use with basic texts which you will use repeatedly. You can make these notes almost anywhere, travelling, waiting for an appointment and so on. You do not require any special equipment other than the text and a highlighting pen and pencil. Unless you find the act of note making helpful in fixing ideas in your memory, there is no special point in making separate notes. Make your notes either by highlighting or writing on the text itself.

1. Highlighting texts

Use a highlighter pen to mark important ideas in the text you are studying. The aim with this method of note making is to mark the text so that you can return to these particular points at a later time and study them more closely. It is useful to highlight words so that you can read them more or less as a sentence. What you underline depends on what your mind is focusing on at the time of reading. Highlighting makes the text your own.

2. Writing on the text

As well as highlighting your own copies of a text, you may also choose to carry on a dialogue with the text that you are reading. You can do this by:

▓ writing comments in the margin agreeing or disagreeing with the author

▓ presenting counter arguments

▓ posing questions

To be able to do this you have to be actively involved in what you read, measuring what the author has written against your own experience and beliefs.

3. Making your own index
The book's own index may not be particularly well constructed, so it may be useful to compile your own index of the passages that are valuable or that you need to reread.

Making separate notes
Rather than writing on the text, you may decide to make separate notes because

▓ you do not want to mark your books

▓ referring to the book later is difficult

▓ a précis of the information is more useful for your purpose

▓ you have only borrowed a copy of the text

The important points to note are as follows.

1. All reference details
Note down the reference details of everything you read. Finding information in the first place can be time consuming; finding it again some time afterwards can sometimes prove impossible.

▓ **You need to record all the details that are needed in the reference** and bibliography section of your written work:

author, title, publisher, date published and page numbers where the details appear. You will need this later on when referencing material for your assignments (see Chapter 10).

▓ **Note down details of texts that have been of no use** to you. This may seem like a waste of time; however, a note to remind yourself of why you decided the work was of no interest is enough to prevent you from tracking down the same piece of work a second time, later on in your studies.

▓ **Use cards to record all the details.** You can then easily sort them into alphabetical order when you come to write your reference sections.

2. Quotations

Note down any useful quotations. If a particular sentence or paragraph strikes you at the time of reading as being a potential quotation, note it carefully. Use quotation marks to indicate the beginning and end of material you have copied exactly. Show clearly if you have left out any word or words by adding three full stops in the appropriate place in the quotation. Record the chapter and page number and file it where you know you are going to be able to find it.

Instead of making notes of quotations, you may find it more useful to photocopy the extract, adding details about its source in the usual way.

3. Summaries of ideas in the text

Making outline notes of chapters can help clarify and re-inforce knowledge and provides useful summaries for reference. It forces you to think because you have to decide what to write down and how to say it.

To make good summary notes from a book you need to have a reasonable grasp of the subject matter, so that you can sort out the important from the less important points. Having a clear idea of what you are looking for prevents you finishing up with large quantities of notes that you made in the hope that amongst them, you will be able to find something that may prove useful.

Once you have developed an understanding of the text, you could create a diagram of the central ideas. Alternatively, you might like to construct a mind map (see Chapter 6) of your reading.

Problems with academic reading

Difficulty in understanding

When you experience difficulties in understanding a text and get stuck, it means you have lost track of the argument. Find ways of reconstructing the argument in your mind:

- **Look back to earlier parts.**

- **Check the title, contents list and introduction** to remind yourself what the writer claimed to be setting out to discuss.

- **Find out what the author thinks are the central ideas.** Look in the preface, foreword and introduction.

- **Reread, look ahead** and see if you can pick up the argument.

- **Read the conclusion** to see where the argument eventually leads.

- **Look at your lecture notes** to see if they can help you shed light on the text.

- **Break up your reading into small pieces.** The benefit of reading section by section is that you pause after each section and consolidate your thoughts.

- **Write notes.** Try to summarize what you have read so far. Writing makes you take hold of the ideas and put them in your own terms.

- **Discuss the text with other people.** Try to reach agreement on the theme. Then discuss differing opinions on aspects such as the central ideas in individual sections and in the material as a whole.

▓ **If all else fails, skip over the difficult sections of the text.** They are seldom essential to what follows. Moving on releases the tension of trying to understand them.

Can't concentrate
This is most likely to happen when you are not reading in a way that best suits your purpose (see Chapter 7). You may need to define your needs more clearly and then be more active in pursuing your purpose.

Disagreement with the text
Many ideas seem implausible when you first come across them. Give yourself a chance to find out what is on offer. Try to write down your criticisms and counter arguments point by point, instead of just feeling irritated. Reacting in this way against what you read can help you sort out your own ideas.

Forgetting the material
The purpose of reading is not to be able to store the whole text in your mind. What you want is to be able to think with the ideas the author has presented. Make notes as a permanent record.

Working with academic texts: key points

▓ Buy your own copies of core texts and customize them by making notes and highlighting.

▓ Don't expect to be able to understand academic texts at the first reading.

▓ Make notes of reference details, quotations and key ideas.

---

9 Improving your writing

This chapter:

- considers the basic tools of writing
- helps you develop your writing style
- gives advice about overcoming some common problems

Improving your writing skills

There are three good reasons why it's worthwhile spending time and effort in improving your ability to write well.

- **It's an extremely useful skill:** to be able to write clearly, simply and in a way that conveys meaning to the reader is probably one of the most useful skills you can have.

- **It's good learning:** in order to be able to put your thoughts on paper, in a way that someone else will understand, you first need to have sorted out your own thoughts. The process of sorting and then writing brings with it new insights and different perspectives. Muddled writing is usually a sign of muddled thinking.

- **You'll do lots of it:** in educational institutions, learning is mostly assessed through written assignments. On a 3 year degree programme, the average student has to submit 50 written assignments totalling approximately 100 000 words (the equivalent of two small books). There may also be up to 30, three hour, written examination papers.

Basic writing tools

Writing is a skill that improves with practice. The following section looks at the main tools for writing. What follow are tips and techniques that other people have found useful. Do remember that there is not one *right* approach to writing that will suit everybody. You need to develop your own style and repertoire for the kind of writing that you do.

1. Words

Good writing requires you to be precise and concise with words. It is hard not to be critical of even a good piece of work, when language is loosely used and words are incorrectly spelt. Readers quickly form unfavourable first impressions and first impressions are notoriously difficult to change.

A dictionary is an essential aid in helping you improve your skill with words. It will help you to:

▓ clarify meaning

▓ extend your vocabulary

▓ improve your spelling

A thesaurus will help you to

▓ select the most appropriate words by showing different shades of meaning

▓ spark new ideas by sending you off on a slightly different track

▓ make emphasis clear, eg by being dramatic, censorious or neutral

A computer spell checker can be useful in helping show words that you have spelt incorrectly. What it cannot do is show where you have spelt a word correctly, but used it incorrectly. (See Appendix D for a list of commonly confused words.) Spell checkers are no substitute for proof reading.

Jargon

The Concise Oxford Dictionary defines jargon as: *'unintelligible words, gibberish; barbarous or debased language; mode of speech full of unfamiliar terms'*. Another way of defining jargon might be *'a useful technical shorthand'*.

Every subject you study will have its own particular vocabulary of concepts and ideas that relate especially to it. However, such specialist vocabularies are likely to exclude a reader who is unfamiliar with the subject.

When you plan to use jargon in your writing, first ask yourself:

▨ *What jargon can I safely assume my reader will know?* These words can then be used without providing an explanation of their meaning.

▨ *With what words will the reader be unfamiliar?* The words on this list will need explanation if your reader is to understand what you write.

▨ *How many jargon words do I intend to use in the whole text?* The answer to this question will help you decide which method of explanation to use.

If you only use a small number of unfamiliar terms you should explain the word when you first you use it, but not on subsequent occasions.

If you plan to use a large amount of jargon, first ask yourself if so much jargon is really necessary. If you decide that it is, provide the reader with a separate glossary of terms. Too many in text explanations of jargon are likely to result in the reader losing the thread of your argument.

2. Grammar

Correctly used, grammar helps your writing to be precise. (Appendix E points out some common grammatical errors.) If you have access to a computer, using a grammar checker will also point out your mistakes and offer possible solutions.

3. Punctuation

Punctuation helps make your meaning clear to the reader. When you are writing a formal piece, avoid using the following:

▓ **exclamation marks and dashes:** they are more suited to an informal style of writing

▓ **brackets:** using brackets implies that the information contained in them is additional to your main point. Decide either to include it as part of the main text, or leave it out

▓ **question marks:** your job is to answer questions, not ask them

4. Sentences

Keep them short
In general use short sentences whenever possible. Research carried out in the USA into sentence length and understanding produced the following results.

▓ 95 per cent of readers understood a sentence with 8 words

▓ 75 per cent of readers understood a sentence of 17 words

▓ Only 4 per cent of readers understood a sentence of 27 words

Leaving 96 per cent of your readers puzzled is not a good idea.

Aim for variety
The shorter your sentences, the more clearly they convey your thinking. However, if you were always to write in short sentences, your writing could lack flow. Longer sentences do have a part to play in good writing, particularly when you are developing an argument.

Consider structure
Before beginning to write a sentence, decide what it is that you want to say. When you have decided on the main point, remember that the first and last words in the sentence get more attention than those in the middle. For maximum impact therefore, place the ideas that you want to emphasize at the beginning or end of the sentence. If you plan to have more than one point in a single sentence, write two sentences. If two points are closely related, use a semicolon.

5. Paragraphs

Each paragraph in your writing should focus on one theme. If you are dealing with a particularly complex or lengthy theme, you may need to divide it into subthemes and devote a paragraph to each of these.

Start with a sentence which indicates the theme of the paragraph. This enables the reader to focus on the subject you are about to present. The sentences which follow should set out your thoughts in an understandable order. In this way, you will be able to guide your reader along the lines of your argument. Make connections between sentences so that your argument is presented fluently. To do this use words or phrases like: *'but'*, *'however'*, *'although'*, *'therefore'*, *'on the other hand'*, *'nevertheless'*, *'not only ... but also'*, *'conversely'*.

These words signpost a change of emphasis and help to move the argument forward.

6. Computers

Many members of staff require you to word process your assignments. If your access to a computer is limited, you may find it easier to work on the draft by hand and type up the final version. If you have your own computer, using it makes drafting easier.

There are advantages and disadvantages to using a word processing package to help improve your writing skills.

Advantages:
- you are able to make changes
- add information later on
- delete information
- have a professional finished product
- run spell and grammar checks
- keep a copy of your work

Disadvantages:
- you need easy access to a machine
- need reasonable typing skills
- can lose text
- composing straight onto a computer can be difficult
- spell checks can give a false sense of security
- the packages do not have technical vocabularies

Getting started

Planning

Time spent planning and structuring your work before you begin to write is time well spent. How much time you dedicate to planning and structuring depends on your own preferred style. Some people do not begin writing until they have a comprehensive written outline of the whole piece. Others prefer to sketch an outline and develop their ideas as they are writing.

Whatever method you adopt, you will need:

▨ an outline so that you can impose an order on your thoughts

▨ a logical sequence for your themes

▨ ideas about how to link the themes together

When writing, use subheadings to guide the reader through your plan. Subheadings will also help you focus on the theme of each section and prevent you wandering off the point.

The reader

It is important to keep your reader in mind when you are writing. The purpose of your writing is to communicate your ideas to another person. If you are unsure about what level to aim at, think of the reader as someone who is familiar with your subject, but without an in depth knowledge. In this way you should avoid talking down to them, by explaining concepts they already understand, or talking over their heads, using too much unexplained jargon.

Writing

Nobody gets it right first time. Assume that your first attempts at writing will not be particularly good and then just start. Once you have begun writing, try to keep up your momentum. Try not to be too critical of what you have written. Think of it as a first draft. Remember that writing is a skill and like all skills it develops with practice.

Developing your style

Developing your own style of writing is a continuous process. You will need different styles, for different kinds of readers and for different academic disciplines.

Be cautious
Be cautious when you write. A common mistake to make in the early stages of developing your writing style is to make sweeping statements. Remember that very little can be said with absolute certainty. For example don't write: *'It is always the case that ...'* instead put *'It is often the case that ...'*. *'This shows that ...'* becomes *'This would appear to show that ...'*.

Recognize that you are unlikely to have the full picture or know all the facts. For example, if you have read five accounts of a particular subject, don't state: *'All writers believe that ...'*. Instead put something like: *'All the writers referenced in this piece agree that ...'*.

Be precise
Precision plays an important part in good writing so avoid generalizations. *'The vast majority of respondents claimed that ...'* becomes *'78 per cent of respondents said that ...'*. *'It has been said that ...'* becomes *'Taylor and Jones said that ...'*.

Be balanced
Write about your ideas in a way that does not show which side you are on. Present both sides of the case in a reasoned and logical way. If you present the case rationally, the force of your points will influence the reader without your needing to include your own bias.

Creative versus critical

There are two different dimensions to writing: a creative dimension and a critical one (Marshall and Rowland, 1993). It is very difficult to combine the two, since the brain is not designed to be able to create and criticize at the same time.

Being creative is the process of capturing on paper your thoughts and ideas. In order to be able to do this, you need to develop a momentum. Being critical of what you write stops the flow. Don't worry about having the best words or phrases for what you want to say, just get down the general idea. If you don't know how to begin your first paragraph, go on to the next one and return to it later.

Being critical is when you read over what you have written and try to improve it. It involves rewording, rearranging and editing what you wrote in the creative phase.

Reviewing your work

If possible, review your work the day after you have written it. Coming fresh to what you have written enables you to see it in a new light. You need to ask yourself:

▓ are the grammar, spelling and punctuation correct?

▓ are the sentences structured clearly?

▓ is there signposting between the sentences and paragraphs?

▓ is the overall structure of the piece logical?

▓ has any necessary jargon been explained?

▓ are there any parts that could be deleted?

▓ have you avoided generalizations?

If you have time, it is useful to get a friend to read your work. Proof reading your own work is difficult, as it is easy to misread a piece with which you are very familiar.

Problems with writing

Unable to get started

Putting ideas down on paper for other people to read and judge can be difficult at the best of times. Knowing that the finished product is going to be formally assessed increases the level of difficulty since there is now the fear of not suc-ceeding. Fear of failure is something that you will have to face. Becoming skilled at writing involves accepting that there may be times when you produce a piece that is not of the required standard. You may decide not to hand in a piece of work because you are worried you might fail. Non sub-mission of work results in a fail grade anyway, so you might as well hand in what you have done. Whatever the outcome, you will receive feedback that will help you learn how to write better. There is also a chance that you will pass. Maybe you are being too critical of your work.

Blocks

When you come up against a block when you are writing, it is usually a good idea to take a break and return to the work later. Alternatively, you could keep working but go on to another section. If deadlines are tight you may simply have to keep going and hope that you will develop some momentum.

Getting feedback

The best way to develop your writing is to practise and get feedback on it.

From other students:
Exchanging work with other people on your course can be extremely valuable. In general, it is less anxiety provoking to receive their comments than those of the tutor. Also, by seeing how someone else has approached the same task, you broaden your own skill area.

When the work has been assessed, if you are disappointed with your grade, find people who got a higher grade. Ask if you can read their work. Pay careful attention to how they approached the task, how they structured their argument and their writing style.

From tutors:
When a piece of work is returned by the tutor, most people's first response is to look at the grade. Depending on what it is, you may feel elated or depressed or somewhere between the two. After looking at the grade, many students simply file the assignment away and never look at the comments that the tutor has written. If you want to develop your writing skills, you need to pay attention to these comments, as they usually contain constructive advice.

Having someone provide detailed comments on your writing is a great learning opportunity. Try not to take the comments personally. In general, tutors tend to write about what you did not do well. There are usually fewer positive comments. Because of this the feedback can seem negative. Even if the work is good, they will usually mention something more that could have been added. Don't dismiss the feedback thinking 'are they never satisfied?'. Remember that most tutors do want you to improve.

Improving your writing: key points

▓ Plan your work before you begin to write.

▓ Don't try to be creative and critical at the same time.

▓ Ask people for feedback.

▓ The more you practise, the better you get.

Reference

Marshall, L. and Rowland, F., *A Guide To Learning Independently*, 2nd edn. Milton Keynes, Open University Press, 1993.

10 Essays and projects

This chapter:

▨ explains how to prepare, write and submit essays and projects

▨ gives details of how to reference material

Part 1: writing essays

What is an essay?

An essay is a short piece of writing on a specific theme. It takes the form of a logically presented argument. A typical essay length is between 1000 and 3000 words. You usually have 5 to 6 weeks to prepare one.

Assessment criteria

Ask your tutor to provide you with a set of the assessment criteria against which your essay will be evaluated. If these are not available, as a general guide, make sure your essay:

▨ answers the question set in the title

▨ draws on relevant material both from the course and from reading

▨ shows evidence of understanding the main concepts used

▨ presents a logical argument

▨ style is analytical, objective and easy to read

Stages of essay writing

There are three different stages to writing an essay:

Stage one: preparation
1. define the task
2. gather the information
3. sort the material

Stage two: writing
1. answer the question
2. present an argument
3. provide evidence
4. review, evaluate and edit

Stage three: submitting
meet the deadline

Stage one: preparation

1. Define the task
Before you begin to gather materials for an essay you need to:

▓ clarify the topic

▓ decide on its scope, that is, what you are trying to achieve

Clarify the topic
A common mistake when writing essays is to misinterpret what the question is asking you to do. No matter how good an essay you produce, if it is not on the right subject, you won't pass.

If you are unclear about what you are required to do, the first person to talk to is your tutor. Don't be put off if no one else is asking for clarification. Being clear about the task will ensure that you focus on what is required. It will also save you time, since you know what to look for in your research.

It is also a good idea to discuss the topic with other people on the course. In this way you can pool, and therefore extend, your thinking about the task.

Define the topic

Once you are clear about the task, you need to decide on its scope. Look carefully at the essay title, word by word. Identify the **process words**, which tell you what you are being asked to do. Figure 5 provides an explanation of some of the most commonly used process words.

Your task is to present an argued case on the topic that you have been set. Do this by thinking about the topic, in the light of what you have been studying.

2. Gather information

By reading

You are expected to read around the essay subject. It is not enough simply to rely on the notes you have taken during lectures. How much reading you do is a matter for your own judgement. You need to do enough to ensure that you know the subject thoroughly. You also need to know when to stop. There will always be more you can read, but you need to allow time to organize your notes and plan and write the essay.

Develop an overview of the topic. First go over your lecture notes to see what might be relevant. Then start your reading. A good place to start is a general text which gives the main points. There will usually be references in the text, which you may want to follow up. It's a bit like a treasure hunt; you move from one clue to the next.

Keep a clear view of the task. When you are tracking down information, it is easy to become interested in a particular topic. You may then wander off the track.

compare:	look for similarities and differences between, give different explanations about why things occur and perhaps reach a conclusion about which is preferable
consider:	present thoughts about
contrast:	look for differences between two or more things
criticize:	give your judgement about the merit of theories, opinions or the truth of facts
define:	set down the precise meaning, examine different definitions
describe:	present a clear, detailed description
discuss:	give the arguments for and against
explain:	give reasons for
illustrate:	make clear by giving examples of
interpret:	make clear the meaning of/reasons for, and usually give your judgement of
outline:	present a description of the most important features
review:	look over an area and assess its strengths and weaknesses
summarize:	present the most important points

Figure 5 Commonly used process words.

By taking notes

While you are reading you need to take notes. Think carefully about the essay title so that you are able to decide what is relevant and therefore what you need to note down. Note down the exact details of the books or articles that you are reading (see later in this chapter for more guidance on this point).

3. Sort the material

Structure the essay

A well-structured essay has:

* **an introduction:** this acts as a map for the reader. It sets out the path that your essay will follow. The introduction:

    sets out the key sections that will be covered in the essay

    explains briefly why you have decided on this particular structure

    gets the reader's attention and interest

* **a body:** here you set out your argument. In the body:

    order your main points in sequence

    link the points logically

    have subsections

    use subheadings, if allowed by your tutor

* **a conclusion:** the conclusion is the last and most important part of your essay. It is worth spending time on writing a good one. Try to avoid writing it when you have run out of energy. If necessary, leave the essay and come back to add the conclusion. The conclusion:

draws together the main points of your essay

sums up the facts and how you have interpreted them

relates to your introduction

shows how the essay has answered the question

where appropriate, looks forward and describes future courses of action

rounds off the essay

doesn't introduce new ideas

Write a basic plan

Deciding on the main sections of your essay, and how they should be arranged, is an important part of the planning process. Don't be tempted to begin writing without a plan and hope that a structure will develop.

Put your reading and notes to one side and begin to write a basic plan. **To write your plan you could:**

- **brainstorm** the ideas that you now have about the topic. Write down all your thoughts as quickly as possible. Once you have dried up, go back and sort them out

- **mind map** the essay topic (see Chapter 6). Do a quick, initial mind map, then go back and develop a more thoughtful one

- **do rough notes.** Write out your ideas; add points for and against; list the questions that you still have. Go back and rewrite the rough notes into a plan

- **cut and paste.** List all your ideas about the subject, then cut the notes into strips and arrange them according to their themes

- **use 'sticky notes'.** Write your ideas on separate sticky notes. Then using a large sheet of paper (or your wall) arrange the notes under themes

Organize your notes

Once you have a basic plan, you can now return to your notes and begin to sort them out. You could:

- **use a coding system:** allocate a number to each of the sections of your plan. Allocate a letter to each of the subsections. When you go through your notes, assign each piece of information a number and letter according to where it fits in your basic plan

- **use note cards:** allocate a card for each section of the essay. Write notes on the cards and arrange them in the sequence of the essay

Remember that this is only a basic plan. When you are writing the essay, you may not follow this plan exactly. As new ideas occur to you, add them to your plan.

Stage two: writing

1. Answer the question

While you are writing your essay, always keep the essay question in mind. This will help you maintain focus and keep on track. It will also help you decide which pieces of information to include and which to leave out. A good essay does not try to cram in everything that you have read.

2. Present an argument

Presenting an argument demonstrates that you can take ideas and make them work for you. To do this you need to sort out your points into a logical order. Each main point should consist of one or more paragraphs.

Signpost

In trying to follow your train of thought, it is easy for the reader to get lost. Use signposting to show clearly how the points link together to form your argument. Indicate where the argument is going, by using signposting words. For example:

'as we have seen'

'in conclusion'

'having covered ..., we now move on to ...'

'to summarize'

Remember you've been researching this subject for a number of weeks. What is an obvious order to you may not be so to your reader. You need therefore to take extra care to explain your thought processes.

Be objective
You need to write in an objective way. Let the facts, not your emotions, do the work for you. Show all sides of the argument, don't just present the parts that reinforce your case. Try to anticipate counter arguments and address these.

3. Provide evidence
You cannot expect your reader to believe something, just because you say it. Show how your thinking has been informed by the reading that you have done. Refer to texts that you have read and give reasons and evidence for what you say. To support your argument, you may also find it useful to quote from some of the texts.

References

When you are discussing a writer's ideas, even if you are not directly quoting them, you need to provide a reference. By giving references you:

§ allow the reader to follow up your information source

§ allow the reader to consider the nature of the source

§ show you have read the literature

There are two systems for referencing, the Harvard and Vancouver styles. You need to check with tutors which they want you to follow. Whatever style you adopt, use the same one for the whole of your essay. Don't mix the two styles in the same piece of work.

Harvard style

In the body of your essay, where you refer to an author's ideas, give the author's name, the year of publication of the text and the page number, for example: (Peat, F.D., 1995, p. 56).

At the end of the essay, give an alphabetical list of all the references you have used. Each reference should include:

§ author's name and initials

§ year or date of publication of the text

§ full title of the text, place of publication

§ publisher

For example:
> Peat, F.D. (1995), *Blackfoot Physics – A Journey into the Native American Universe*. London, Fourth Estate Limited.

Vancouver style

This system gives the same information as in the Harvard system, but refers the reader to a numbered footnote or end-note.

For example: Peat.[1]

    1. Peat, F.D. *Blackfoot Physics – A Journey into the Native American Universe*. London, Fourth Estate Limited, 1995.

When using the Vancouver system, providing an alphabetical list of all your references at the end of the essay is optional.

Where to find reference details

▨ **Books:** you can usually find most of the information at the front of the book, on the page following the title page. If there are two or three authors of the same work, you need to note the names of all of them. If there are more than three authors, note the first one then write *et al*, a Latin abbreviation for 'and others'.

▨ **Journals:** when referencing journal articles you will need to give details of: the author, year of publication, title of article, title of journal, volume number and month. This information can usually be found on the contents page.

▨ **The Internet:** when referencing material from the Internet and other electronic sources, you need to give: the author's name, the author's Internet address if available, title or title line of message, title of the complete work or title of the list/site, Internet address and date if available. For example:

    Sherman, D., [100479.100@compuserve.com], *London Stock Exchange launches second Big Bang*

    [http:/www.pathfinder.com@@*18gpwUAdCw7m@yo /money/latest/RB/1997Oct19/281.htm]

It is useful to note the details of your reading on index cards. You can then arrange the cards into alphabetical order when you need to write out your list of references.

Bibliography

As well as a reference list, you may also include a bibliography. This is an alphabetical list of the other information sources you read, but did not refer to specifically in the essay.

Quotations

Try to avoid using too many quotations, since the aim of essay writing is to express ideas in your **own** words. Quotations can however be useful when:

* concepts need exact definitions

* the exact words express ideas in a particular way

* you need to be clear about the writer's own words before you can begin an evaluation

You must use quotation marks. If you leave out some of the writer's words, show you have done this by inserting three dots. If you add anything to the original quotation, include the additional information within square brackets. Following the quotation, give the same reference details as described above. For example: *'Thus, to the earliest peoples ... knowledge and knowing had more to do with a discriminating perception of the mind and the senses* [rather] *than with the accumulation of facts.'* (Peat, F.D., 1995, p.56)

Plagiarism

Plagiarism is taking and using another person's ideas and thoughts and presenting them *as if they were your own*. Plagiarism is taken very seriously by tutors and usually leads to a formal disciplinary process. **Plagiarism is:**

▓ copying passages from texts, journals and other materials and not providing references for them

▓ copying from another student's work and presenting it as if it were your own

Plagiarism is not:
▓ including quotations and referencing them

▓ discussing ideas with other members of your group and including the results of your discussions in your own work

Tutors can usually easily detect plagiarism. The text that has been copied will probably be familiar to the tutor. Also the difference in the writing styles is usually obvious.

4. Review, evaluate and edit
When you have completed the first draft of your essay, you need to review, evaluate and edit what you have written. Ask yourself:

▓ *Does this answer the question?*

▓ *Is the argument presented logically?*

▓ *Is all the material relevant?*

▓ *Are the references and footnotes correct?*

▓ *Is it within the stated word limit?*

▓ *Is the style appropriate?*

In addition, use the guidelines given above about essay structure as a check list to ensure that you have covered all the main points. Make any changes that are necessary. Finally proof read the essay to check your spelling and grammar.

Stage three: submitting

Make sure that you know the procedure for submitting work. It could, for example, involve handing in your work to a course administrator, who date stamps it and gives you a receipt. Don't be tempted to shortcut this procedure. Handing work to your tutor in a corridor might seem like a good idea, but it is easy for tutors to misplace a single piece of work handed to them 'on the run'.

Always take a copy of work that you are submitting. Work can go missing but this is less of a problem if you have a copy.

Deadlines and extensions
Be sure that you hand in your work before the deadline or you may be penalized (see Chapter 3). If you are unable to submit your work on time, it is sometimes possible to get an extension to the deadline. These are usually only given for serious reasons, for example if you have been certified sick by your doctor or you have had some serious personal problem.

There will be a formal procedure that you must follow when applying for an extension. All of the procedures require you to set out your case in writing and provide supporting documentation as evidence.

Part 2: writing project reports

There are a number of different forms of project that you might be asked to write, for example:

▓ a research project

▓ a long essay

▓ a problem solving project

The three stages of preparation, writing and submission are similar in many ways to those for writing essays. The preparation and submission stages are almost the same. The writing stage, is, however, different from essay writing, except for the last part: review, evaluate and edit.

Stage one: preparation	1. define the task
	2. gather the information
	3. sort the material
Stage two: writing	1. focus on the aims and objectives
	2. follow a report structure
	3. use an appropriate style
	4. review, evaluate and edit
Stage three: submitting	meet the deadlines

Stage one: preparation

1. Define the task
Clarify the topic and decide the scope of the project in the same way as you would for an essay.

2. Gather the information
Complete the reading. In addition you may need to carry out some primary research. This requires you to gather your own data and analyse and interpret it yourself. You could do this for example, by distributing a questionnaire, completing a survey or carrying out a number of interviews.

3. Sort the material
Projects have a tightly structured format and so mistakes are more obvious than in an essay. You need to be clear about what goes into the different sections. Ask your tutors for

guidelines on how the final report should be structured. The following is a generally acceptable format:

title page

contents page

summary

aim and purpose

introduction

methodology

findings

analysis and discussion

conclusions

recommendations

appendices

references

bibliography

Title page
This should include:

▓ a title that is brief and to the point and which accurately describes what the report is about. For example: *A report on the catering provision provided by the college* is a better title than *The college canteen*. You can give the report a sub-title, if it clarifies what the study is about

▓ name of the writer

▓ submission date

Contents page

This is a directory of your report. It details the page numbers and the names and numbers of the sections and subsections. You cannot complete the contents page until you have written the final report.

Summary

The summary can be referred to either as an _abstract, summary_ or _executive summary_. The summary gives the reader an immediate overview of the report. It should be very brief. For example a report of 10 000 words should only have a summary of approximately 400 words. It is the last thing that you write, but it appears at the beginning of the report. The summary describes:

▓ the problem you investigated

▓ the methods used

▓ the conclusions reached

▓ any recommendations you make

Aim and purpose

This is an explanation of the aim, objectives and purpose of the report and the area that the report will cover. **The aim** is a broad general statement of what you intend to do. **The objectives** provide more specific statements of what has to be done to achieve the aim. Useful words to begin objectives are: _analyse, calculate, define, describe, develop, establish, evaluate, identify, measure, monitor, plan._

Introduction

This defines the scope of the report. This is one of the last sections that you write since your ideas will grow and develop as you work through and write up your materials. It details:

▓ the issue or problem

▓ the context and background of the report

▓ why the problem is seen as important

▓ why the project was written

Methodology

This section is sometimes called *procedure*. It should give enough information for another person to be able to repeat your research. It explains

▓ what methods you used to gather information, for example, any interviews you carried out, documents and articles studied, field work

▓ when and where you carried out your investigation

▓ details of techniques you employed, for example, how many people you questioned, what questions were asked. You should include copies of any questionnaires used, lists of interview questions asked, etc, in the appendix.

Findings

The findings contain the detailed information that you gathered during the project. Group the information together and classify it under a number of headings and subheadings. Use as many subsections as required, giving each its own heading. The findings only contain factual information. Do not include any of your own opinions or draw any conclusions at this stage.

Analysis and discussion

This is your opportunity to evaluate and interpret the information you collected. Present the picture that has emerged from your study. Now you can say what you think, based on findings in the main body. Before you write this section, you need to read through the whole report and note the key points.

Conclusions

This presents a clear summary of the findings and analysis and draws conclusions. Do not introduce any new facts at this stage of the report.

Recommendations

You may not always have a recommendations section in your project report. If, however, the project was a practical problem that you investigated, then you are expected to include recommendations. These are suggestions about how the problem can be addressed and what actions may need to be taken in the future. The recommendations should arise logically from the work you have been doing. Recommendations should be:

▓ realistic

▓ practicable

▓ in a logical order or prioritized

Appendices

You should aim to avoid cluttering the main body of the report with too much detail. Any information which is relevant and interesting, but not essential to the reader's understanding of the report, should be numbered in the order in which it is referred to in the project and included in an appendix. The reader can then choose to read this section or leave it out.

The kind of information that might go into an appendix might be:

▓ detailed charts

▓ tables of figures

▓ sets of interview questions

▓ a copy of any questionnaire used, but not completed ones

References and bibliography
Set these out in the same way as for an essay.

Stage two: writing

1. Keep a focus on the aims and objectives of your project
Because of the length of the document, it is easy to forget what you are trying to achieve.

2. Follow a report structure
Group the material under suitable headings and present it in a logical order. Link the different sections together. If you can, use diagrams, tables, figures to get a point over more quickly than words. Label and number all diagrams and tables, for example: Figure 1 ..., Figure 2 ...

Use the decimal system of numbering illustrated in Figure 6. Simple numbering is not usually followed in reports since, although it does identify each of the paragraphs, it does not show the logical sequence of ideas. Use these section numbers when referring to parts of the main body in your conclusion.

3. Use a report writing style
- **Make the report easy to read:** write simply and clearly, keeping paragraphs short. Allow plenty of space. The more space there is between sections, the easier it is for your reader to digest the information.

- **Use a tone that is appropriate** to your reader and the purpose of your report. In general, the tone should be neutral, plain and precise since individuality would divert the reader's attention away from the report.

- **Be factual and objective:** your writing style should be without prejudice or emotion.

1. Section headings	Main sections of the report. For example:
	
	1. Introduction
	  2. Methodology
	  3. Findings
	  and so on.

1.1 Subsections	The first decimal number is used for the major subheadings within each main section.

1.1.1 Paragraph numbers	As each section is developed, each paragraph is given a number with an additional decimal point.
	    1.1.2
	    1.1.3
	    1.1.4 etc

1.2	Once a topic has been fully discussed, the next number is used, showing that a new subsection has started.

Figure 6 Decimal numbering system for report writing.

▓ **Signpost:** the longer the report, the easier it is for the reader to get lost and lose focus. The more need there is, therefore, to signpost the links between the different sections.

▓ **Word length:** You will have been given guidelines about the length of your project. If you have not been told the word length, ask. If you have been set a maximum word length, don't exceed this, as you may be penalized.

4. Review, evaluate and edit
In the same way that you would when writing an essay.

Stage three: submitting

Find out if you need to submit a typed report or whether a hand written one is acceptable. If you are typing the report, it is usual to do this in 1.5 or double spacing. Quotations should be indented and in single spacing.

Essays and projects: key points

▓ Clarify what you have been asked to do and then collect the necessary information.

▓ Decide on a logical structure following an appropriate format.

▓ Provide all the necessary reference details.

▓ Read through and edit the finished piece.

▓ Hand in your work on time.

---

11 Working in groups

This chapter:

- outlines the benefits of working in groups
- gives ideas for improving your group working skills
- explains how to set up your own learning group
- gives advice about working in a project group

During your programme of study, you will probably spend some time working in groups. You may decide to set up your own group to help with studying or you may be required to work in groups as part of your course work assessment.

Why work in groups?

Working in groups:

- **promotes your learning**
  Explaining, discussing and teaching others what you know is one of the best ways of increasing your own understanding of a subject.

- **develops your ability to work cooperatively with others**
  In groups you learn to:

  work participatively with others

  present and defend your ideas

admit when you don't know something

criticize other people's ideas without offending them

accept criticism yourself

become more tolerant and less extreme in your opinions

░ **helps build your self confidence and develop skills you will need in the future**

░ **produces better solutions than can be generated by one person working alone**
A group is good at working on complex problems. It can bring together a number of different people with a wide range of skills, ideas and view points.

░ **helps you learn to manage the challenges involved in working with others**
Working in groups is not always straightforward. One of the benefits lies in the range of approaches that it offers. When you need to agree a single way of working, this strength can, however, create difficulties. Different people have different ideas about how things should be done. Learning to manage these differences and being able to use them creatively to produce better solutions is one of the challenges of group working. Conflicts and disagreements can arise. Working in a group offers you the opportunity to learn strategies to cope with competition, defensive and dominant behaviours and to consider issues of leadership and control. All of these are essential skills.

Aspects of group working

There are two aspects to working in a group:

1. The task: getting the work done
This includes:

▓ deciding who will do the work

▓ developing ideas

▓ gathering, sharing and interpreting the information

▓ developing solutions

2. The process: how the group works together
This includes:

▓ improving relationships

▓ managing and resolving conflict

▓ ensuring that everyone is able to contribute

In fact everything that goes on in the group besides getting the job done.

To be effective, and produce a high standard of work, a group needs to develop a full range of both task and process skills. Most people can see the importance of having skills to ensure that the work gets done. Some people, however, think that time spent doing anything other than the task is time wasted. For example, they may come late to a meeting because they say that all the group does at the start of the meeting is *chatter*. They do not understand that *chatter* plays an important part in developing group process skills.

How a group works together affects the end product. Time spent considering how you are working as a group is time well spent. A group that is working well will, for example:

▓ produce a report that does not show where different people have written different sections

▓ do a presentation that is clearly a joint effort, with all group members playing their part, supporting each other and answering questions

When you are working in groups, from time to time, use the following check list to see that all the task and process functions are being carried out. If they are not, discuss how the group can improve. If, for example, you discover that you have lost sight of your group deadline, it now becomes everybody's responsibility to be aware of time scales.

Task: getting the work done

generate creative and original ideas

turn ideas into actions

be aware of the need to deliver on time

push the group on to achieve its objectives

search out errors and omissions

judge accurately

bring in new ideas and information

solve difficult problems

Process: how the group works together

coordinate the group's efforts

listen

consider all opinions

build on ideas and suggestions

ensure all opinions are heard

ensure there is a good decision making process

prevent interpersonal conflict

reduce anxiety

Improving your own group working skills

Learn to compromise
Working in a group inevitably means compromise. You probably won't get your own way. Remember that the concessions you make are likely to result in a better final solution.

Encourage others to contribute
Use your skills of active listening (see Chapter 5). Try to involve all group members, especially the quiet ones. Use eye contact, put questions to them directly, make your own points of view in the form of questions rather than statements and ensure that everybody is involved in decision making.

Be objective
Try not to let your feelings towards another person influence your thinking about their ideas. Try not to defend your own ideas just because they are yours.

Show commitment
Contribute energy, commitment and care to whatever you do. If you agree to do something, make sure that you do it. Attend all the group meetings.

Create a supportive atmosphere
Be responsive and appreciative of different points of view and contributions. Ask for other people's views and listen to what they say.

Setting up a learning group

Setting up your own learning group is an excellent way to help you with your studies. It offers all the benefits of working in groups, but avoids the difficulties that are associated with working together on a single piece of work. In a learning group you are all working on your own individual pieces of work, so there is, for example, no need to agree a joint plan of action, or spend time trying to reach consensus decisions.

Learning groups are therefore not only useful in helping you with your studies, they also provide a safe environment within which you can develop your group working skills.

How to set up a learning group

▓ **Find a small group of people who are interested in meeting regularly** to help each other with their work. Keep the group small, about five or six people, or you won't have enough time to get through everybody's work at each meeting.

▓ **Agree when and where to hold your first meeting.** This meeting will be to discuss how you all want to work together as a group.

At the first meeting

Spend some time getting to know each other

If you don't know everybody there, start by introducing yourselves. Then spend some time talking about yourselves and your interests. It does not really matter what you talk about, anything you say will help the other members of the group get to know you. You are going to be working together, the more you know about each other, the more effective the group will be.

Talk about how you want to work together

Discuss what each of you wants to get out of being a member of the group and how you want to work together. You could, one at a time, talk about your own ideas and then follow this with a general discussion to agree a common set of aims.

Agree some ground rules
After you have all heard everybody's ideas about how they would like the group to operate, agree a set of ground rules about how you all want people to behave at meetings. The following are examples of ground rules your group might adopt.

Group members: Attend meetings regularly.

Don't interrupt people when they are speaking.

Have equal time to discuss work.

etc

You don't need a long list of ground rules, just a few basic ones that will help everyone get the most from working together. Write down your ground rules and refer back to them from time to time at future meetings. Check that the rules are still relevant and that you are all observing them.

Decide about future meetings
You need to agree:

▓ how long the meetings should last

▓ where to hold them

▓ when to hold the next meeting

At the second meeting

Begin working in the way that you want to continue.

Allocate your time

Divide the meeting time equally between the people present. For example, if the group is meeting for 2 hours and there are five people present, you could divide your time as follows:

10 minutes:	check in (see below)
20 minutes each:	individual time
10 minutes:	review how the group has worked
Total:	120 minutes

Agree on someone who will act as time keeper for the meeting, to let people know when their time is up. It is a good idea to give a warning a few minutes before people's time is over, so that they can sum up what has been discussed and maybe develop actions that they want to take.

Check in

Spend two or three minutes each at the start of the meeting checking in. This involves each person telling the rest of the group how they are feeling. The reason for checking in is to get some understanding of what has been happening to each person in the group recently. This helps you work together with greater understanding of each other.

Checking in is not having a conversation. Each person just makes a statement, without comments from other people and then the next person begins. You could use the following format for checking in. Each person thinks about three things that have happened to them recently, one for each of the following categories: a trauma, a trivia and a joy. Then, one at a time, you tell each other your trauma, trivia and joy.

Focus on your work, one at a time

Agree an order for people's time, for example who is going first, second, third, and so on. This will avoid time wasting during the meeting as you try to agree who is going next.

When it is your turn, tell the group how you want to use your time. Whatever you want to do is fine: this is **your time**. Other people will spend their time in whatever way they find useful. You don't have to have their agreement on what you do. Don't worry about seeming to be selfish; everybody will have time to do their own work. When it comes to their time, you will give your full concentration to them, so it is all right to expect their concentration on your work. You might want to:

▓ talk through your ideas for your latest piece of work

▓ ask if anyone can explain a difficult concept to you

▓ get people to give you feedback on your written work

If you want feedback on written work, for future meetings, it is a good idea to let people have copies of your work in advance, so that people don't have to read the work during your time.

If, during your time, people seem to be moving away from what you want, let them know. There is no point in sitting there quietly listening, if it is not what you want. This time is valuable for your learning, use it well.

Review how the group worked

At the end of the meeting, spend a few minutes reviewing how you worked together. You may want to consider some of the following aspects of group working:

▓ *Did you observe the ground rules?*

▓ *Did you keep to time?*

▓ *How effective are you in helping each other learn?*

▓ *Do you have any ideas about how the group might work better next time?*

▓ *Do you want to give feedback to the group or to individuals?*

You might find it useful to write down some of the points made during the review. You can then reread them at the start of your next meeting so you can increase the group's effectiveness.

Working in a project group

As part of your course work you may be required to work in a project group. Some of the stages involved are the same as for setting up your own learning groups. There are also some differences, because of the need to produce a single piece of group work.

Agree when and where to hold the first meeting. At the first meeting:

▓ Spend some time getting to know each other

▓ Talk about how you want to work together

▓ Agree some ground rules

Your ground rules for working in a project group might cover such things as:

▓ listening actively

▓ not interrupting each other

▓ the importance of everyone attending meetings

▓ the need for everyone to do an equal share of the work

It is worth spending some time clarifying what the ground

rules mean and gaining everyone's commitment to them.

Project group meetings are often more effective if they have a chairperson. The chairperson's job is to ensure that an agenda is set at the start of the meeting. An **agenda** states:

▓ the items to be discussed

▓ the decisions to be made

▓ the areas of work to be reviewed

The chairperson also needs to make sure that everyone gets a chance to voice ideas and ensure that all of the necessary items are discussed. It is a good idea for all of you to take turns in chairing the meetings, rather than simply relying on one person to do this all the time. This involves:

▓ **At the start of the meeting, deciding on your agenda** if you have not already done so.

▓ **Making notes of the actions as they are agreed**, together with the name of the person who is responsible for the action and the date by which it should be done.

▓ **Towards the end of the meeting, summarizing and reviewing what has taken place.** Review also how the group is working together. You could ask each person to name two things that helped the group work together and two things that hindered it. At the next meeting the group needs to be particularly careful to avoid these hindering behaviours.

Sample group timetable

Figure 7 shows a sample timetable for your group working. It assumes that you have four group meetings in the course of working on your project. It lists the activities that the group needs to carry out at each stage.

Meeting 1

※ Clarify the task.
※ Generate ideas about how best to do it.
※ Allocate tasks to group members.
※ Share out fairly the tasks no-one wants to do.
※ Clarify project deadlines.
※ Agree time limits for completing the tasks.

Between meetings: individuals carry out work.

Meeting 2

※ Present and discuss information that has been gathered.
※ Generate solutions. This may take some time as you will need to evaluate each suggestion.
※ Turn ideas into actions, breaking the tasks into manageable stages.
※ Allocate tasks to group members.

Between meetings: individuals carry out work.

Meeting 3

※ Monitor progress, see how far members have progressed with their tasks.
※ Reallocate tasks where necessary.

Between meetings: individuals carry out work.

Meeting 4

※ Produce a draft of the final report or presentation.
※ Review draft and make any necessary changes.

Figure 7 Sample project group timetable.

Improving the group process

Use the following set of questions as a checklist to help you develop into an effective project group.

Checklist

▪ Is everyone clear what the group has to do? Do all members accept/approve the objectives? It is a good idea, from time to time, to review and discuss the objectives.

▪ Do group members know what is expected of them and what contributions they each make to the group?

▪ Does the group meet frequently enough? Regular meetings help cohesion and communication.

▪ What problems are there? Are they brought into the open and dealt with? If you can acknowledge your problems and see them as learning opportunities, you should be able to cope with most of the difficulties that arise.

▪ Are standards set and maintained?

▪ Do group members share responsibilities, not leaving everything to one or two group members?

▪ Are relationships within the group good?

▪ Is there good communication between group members?

▪ Do members trust and support each other?

▪ Are disagreements dealt with openly and constructively?

▪ Are individual skills recognized and used as appropriate?

Problems in working in groups

If you pay attention to building cooperation and collaboration within your group there should be few problems, as team members will recognize the benefits of working together. However, no matter how hard the group tries to involve everyone, sometimes a group member does not contribute sufficient work and this can impair the quality of the group's work. If this happens, meet in your whole group to identify the cause of the problem and agree a solution. Make sure that the person concerned is part of these discussions. You could, for example, set the individual some work to complete to an agreed deadline. If the work is not completed, you may need to take further action.

Discuss the problem with your tutor. You may be asked to write a brief group report outlining the contribution made by each person. Each group member should sign the report to indicate that they have read it and agree with the contents.

Working in groups: key points

▓ Plan how you will use the time during meetings.

▓ Pay attention to how the group is working as well as to getting the work completed.

▓ Remember that all groups take time, effort and commitment to become effective.

---

12 Making presentations

This chapter details the five stages involved in presentations:

- stage 1: structuring
- stage 2: planning
- stage 3: rehearsing
- stage 4: presenting
- stage 5: reviewing

You may be asked to give an oral presentation for a number of reasons:

- to start off a discussion in group situations
- as an exercise to help you develop communication skills
- as a method of assessment

You may be given a subject or asked to select a topic that is relevant to a particular area that you are studying. You may give the presentation yourself or work with a partner or a group of your colleagues.

Stage 1: structuring

Find out about your audience

Before you begin preparing your presentation, you need answers to the following questions:

▦ **Who are the audience?** You need to find out about your audience. You need to know who you will be speaking to and what they already know about the subject, so that you can vary the contents of your talk accordingly.

▦ **What is the aim of the presentation?** The objective of any talk or presentation is usually to influence the audience. You either want to persuade them to adopt your point of view or inform them, so that they change their understanding of the subject. Whatever your aim, you need to put your ideas across in a clear and interesting way.

Find out how long the presentation should be

If no time limit is given, aim to talk for no more than 10–15 minutes, as this is the limit of most people's attention span. If you have to give a longer presentation, break it up, to help keep the audience's attention.

Prepare your material

It is never a good idea to improvise a presentation on the day. The lack of planning always shows. Even if the work is not going to be assessed, if you plan and prepare what you are going to say, you will get more out of the exercise and be less nervous on the day.

Decide how to construct your argument

Before you begin to do your research, clarify the main aspects of the topic. Try not to be too ambitious in what you intend to cover. You usually only have time to outline the topic and make a few main points.

Find out whether you have enough facts and ideas on which to build an argument, if not you will need to supplement these with research. Study the facts and ideas that you have and decide how you want to present your case. You may decide to present:

- a fair and impartial account of the evidence and leave your audience to make up their own minds
- the arguments for and against a particular subject
- a case supporting or condemning one particular point of view

Present a clear line of argument

State your arguments clearly and simply. It is important that the audience is able to follow your point of view. Don't think that something is too obvious to need stating. If you do this, you may leave out an essential step in your argument.

Your listeners should be able to move confidently with you from one point to another and know where they are in your argument. You may decide that one side of the argument is stronger and gains your support. You will probably therefore want to emphasize the merits of this view and support it in your conclusion.

Be persuasive

If the point of the presentation is to win support, you need to present your case as persuasively as possible. However, if there are arguments against your own case, do not ignore them. Treat counter arguments objectively and balance them against points of your own, which you consider have more weight.

Give examples and evidence

Examples
One way of being persuasive is to give examples to support

your point of view. Examples are not the same as evidence: they illustrate rather than prove a point. They show people the relevance of the points you are making and help people understand.

Evidence
When you use evidence, state the source of your facts. Balance your own observations against other sources of evidence, for example statistical data, expert analysis and so on. The greater your range of evidence, the more powerful your argument will be.

Stage 2: planning

You have spent a good deal of time researching and thinking about your material. Your audience, however, is probably not as well informed as you, so you need to present them with the main points in a clear and simple way. It is always better to get across a few points well than attempt to cover too much ground. To help you decide what to include, it is often recommended that material is sorted into information:

▓ the audience *must be* given

▓ the audience *should be* given if possible

▓ that would be *useful but which is not vital*

Plan the presentation following the old prescription for a good speech:

▓ *tell them what you are going to say* (introduction)

▓ *tell them* (main body)

▓ *tell them what you have told them* (conclusion)

The introduction
In the introduction you need to include:

▓ an outline of what will be covered in the presentation

▓ the structure you will follow

▓ the objectives and purpose of your presentation

The way you begin your presentation should gain the audience's attention and make them want to know more. A quotation can sometimes be used effectively as an attention-getter.

The main body
Here you should develop your argument logically. Make clear when you are moving from one point to another by using signposts. For example: *'My second reason for ...'*. *'Moving on to consider ...'*.

The conclusion
When you are closing your presentation:

▓ briefly sum up the main points

▓ try to move on to some new, but relevant ground

▓ leave the audience with a new idea to think about

It is important that you have a definite end to the presentation so the audience knows you have finished. You could say something like: *'That concludes my presentation. I am now happy to answer your questions'*.

Prepare cue cards

Do not write out the whole speech word for word or learn it off by heart, since this does not sound very natural. Note down the main points to be covered and write them on small cue cards. There are a number of advantages for using cue cards. Cue cards:

▓ force you to note only the main points and so prevent you from reading large sections of the presentation

▓ make it is easier to find your place when glancing at them

▓ are easier to hold than sheets of paper

▓ don't rustle and make a noise when you turn them over

Tie the cards loosely together so that even if you are nervous and drop them, the cards do not get out of order.

Prepare your visual aids

Illustrations and diagrams often make a point more clearly than words can. Before using them, work out exactly what you want from your visual aids and try to make them as interesting as possible.

There are a number of visual aids that can help you get your message across: booklets, flipcharts, wallcharts, whiteboards, overhead projector transparencies (OHTs), slides, photographs or any combination of these. Flipcharts and OHTs are two of the most frequently used visual aids.

Flipcharts
These are reasonably portable and enable you to prepare sheets in advance. They can also be used briefly during the presentation, for example to note down questions. Avoid writing flipcharts during your presentation, since doing this means that you have to stand with your back to the audience and breaks rapport.

Overhead projector transparencies (OHTs)
There are particularly useful at the start and end of your presentation. At the start you can use them to show the basic

structure of your talk. At the end, you can use them to highlight two or three issues that have arisen. Don't, however,
spend too much time producing elaborate OHTs, when simple ones would get the message across as clearly.

Stage 3: rehearsing

You must rehearse your material. You might also want to
tape or video record your presentation as you rehearse it.
Rehearsing will help you:

▓ get a clear idea of how long the presentation will take

▓ know the presentation well enough to be able to use your
  cue cards

▓ feel less anxious when doing the actual presentation

▓ improve the way you communicate your material

Run through what you intend to say and practise working
from the cue cards. Time your talk. You may need to delete
some of the material to keep within the time limit. Practise
using your visual aids to ensure you are familiar with how
they work.

Think about how you communicate your message

To improve the way you communicate your message, you
need to be aware of what is involved in the communication
process. There are three elements to the process of verbal
communication: the words you use, the way you say the
words and your body language. These three elements make
up the following percentages of the total communication
process:

words	= 7 per cent
way	= 38 per cent
body language	= 55 per cent

Words

Much of the time you spend preparing for a presentation is taken up with deciding what you are going to say and how you will structure the argument. However, no matter how well you have prepared what you are going to say, it is only a small part of the total process involved in communicating your message.

Way

Speak clearly so the audience can hear what you are saying. Pay attention to the way you are speaking:

- Ensure that there is variety in the way you speak. Some people speak in a monotone, where all the words sound the same. Listening to a monotone acts a little like hypnosis and can cause the audience to become sleepy.

- Be aware of the speed of delivery of your presentation. Most of us find listening difficult (see Chapter 6) and many of us speak more quickly when we are nervous. Pace your presentation and slow down when you are covering difficult facts and concepts.

Body language

The non verbal messages that you give through your body language form more than half of the total communication process. During the presentation, therefore, you need to take care that you do not give any non verbal messages that are inconsistent with your presentation. You will feel nervous, but it is not a good idea to communicate this to the audience as it will get in the way of their concentrating on what you have to say.

▓ **Eye contact:** make eye contact with all of the audience as you progress through your presentation. It helps establish rapport and shows you are interested in them.

▓ **Facial expression:** avoid frowning. Smile and look confident, especially at the start of the presentation.

▓ **Gestures:** hand gestures can be used to support meaning and reinforce the message. Don't deliberately use gestures if you would not normally do so, this always looks unconvincing. However, do avoid irritating mannerisms as they distract the audience from what you are saying.

▓ **Barriers:** try to avoid standing behind a table, even though it might make you feel more comfortable. If there is a physical barrier between you and the audience it will be more difficult to establish rapport. Find a way of standing or sitting that makes you feel reasonably comfortable, but still looks open and responsive.

Plan your 'stage'

Think where to place furniture like the table, chairs, overhead projector and flipchart stand. Practise using your visual aids.

Plan the question and answer session

Decide when the audience can ask questions. On the whole it is easier to finish your presentation before responding to questions. Taking questions during the presentation may help in keeping the group's attention, but it could interrupt your flow and result in your running over time.

Anticipate problems

If you are worried or nervous about the presentation, try to imagine the worst thing that could happen. Then go on to plan how you would cope with the situation.

Stage 4: presenting

Arrive early
You will have prepared your material in advance, but also remember to make arrangements to see the room and have a practice run through. Double check the equipment that you intend to use and the layout of the room. Try out the overhead projector and check that it is in focus and that it does not block the audience's view of the screen.

Everyone is nervous when they do presentations. Before you begin, take a few deep breaths. Remember to smile, nervous people tend to frown. If the thought of all those eyes on you makes you anxious, use a visual aid to distract attention from yourself.

Be self-confident
If you have confidence in yourself, the audience will have confidence in you. If you are convinced that you have something of real value to communicate, you will get through to your audience. Don't apologize for your own lack of ability or for the subject of your talk. It is your presentation and if you are well prepared, all should go well. If you haven't prepared thoroughly, it is too late to have second thoughts at this stage.

Beginning the presentation
The first few minutes are the hardest. Once you get going, it becomes easier. Remember to:

- say who you are
- say what you are going to talk about
- ensure that the audience can hear
- check that the audience can see the visual aids
- indicate the structure of the presentation

▨ indicate your attitude to the topic

You need to let the audience know at the start of the presentation when they can ask questions. If someone asks a question during the presentation and you are not ready to answer it, tell them that you will come back to their question at the end.

Making mistakes

Any mistakes you make in your presentation that you think are glaringly obvious to the audience, will probably not even be noticed by them. What seems like an endless pause to you, probably seems only moments to the audience, if they notice at all.

▨ If you lose your place, say something like: *'I seem to have lost my place, can you bear with me for a few seconds'*, then look at your cue cards, take a deep breath and carry on.

▨ If you forget what you were saying, ask the audience to help you. They generally respond very well when you say something like: *'I've totally lost my train of thought. Can anyone remind me where I was?'*.

▨ If you are asked a question that you do not know the answer to, say so. Don't try and bluff your way through.

▨ If you do not understand a question you have been asked, do not ask for it to be repeated, they will do just that and you will be none the wiser. Say: *'I don't follow your question. Can you expand a little on what you are asking?'*

Stage 5: reviewing

At the end of the presentation you might want to get some feedback from the audience. You could ask each person to write down one thing you did well and one area for improvement. Ask them to comment on the content and style of the presentation. Getting feedback in writing and reviewing it later means that you will probably be more responsive to what they say than if they had given it straight after the presentation.

One of the best ways of getting feedback on your presentation is by making a video recording of it. You will need to watch the video at least twice for it to be of use. Once, on your own, to get over the embarrassment of seeing yourself and a second time to be more objective about how well you did. Many people who think they did not do a good presentation are pleasantly surprised when they watch themselves on video. They realize they did considerably better than they thought.

Treat the whole exercise as a learning experience. If you have made mistakes, think how you can improve on your presentation techniques for the next time you present.

13 Preparing for exams

This chapter

▨ looks at the requirements of different kinds of examinations

▨ explains how to prepare for them

▨ helps you cope with exam anxiety

What do you have to do in exams?

The answer to this question may seem obvious: to do well in exams you need to give good answers to the questions that have been set. What is involved in giving a good answer may not, however, be quite so obvious. A good answer will usually show evidence of your ability to:

▨ **Use the course material:** the exam is a test of your understanding of the course you have been studying, not a test of your general knowledge. You are expected to use material from the course as evidence to back up your argument and to show that you know what others have said on the subject.

▨ **Demonstrate your thinking and understanding about the subject area:** any end of course exam is set up as an opportunity to demonstrate that you have worked on and thought about the content of the course. Most of this thinking needs to be done in advance of the exam itself. During the exam you need to put ideas to work, select useful material and answer specific questions.

▩ **Think on your feet:** in an exam you have to perform at a specified time and place, and satisfy the requirements of someone you may not know. You have to think on your feet and get it right first time. Some questions will not be straightforward and may not come in the format that you expected. You therefore have to be prepared to think how to answer the question and select and organize relevant parts of your knowledge.

▩ **Communicate clearly:** you need to answer clearly the questions that have been set. This involves interpreting correctly what you are being asked to do. Examiners also expect your handwriting to be legible and your sentences, paragraphs and essays to be well constructed.

Different types of examinations

Figure 8 gives details of the different types of exams that you may have to take. As you can see, different types of exam test different things and so need different kinds of preparation. In the following sections there are:

▩ **general preparation techniques** that you need whatever kind of exam you are taking

▩ **specific techniques** that are appropriate for different types of exam

General preparation for exams

1. Start your preparations early

Long term preparation for exams involves keeping up with your work **as you go along**. This is even more important if you are to be examined on the work of all of the previous year, or even the previous 2 years. Develop the systematic approach to your studies that is recommended in earlier chapters:

* plan your studies
* do class preparation and follow up
* make good notes
* develop your writing skills.

If you do this, when you come to revision it really will be *revision* and not learning your subjects from scratch. If you have already learnt the material thoroughly, your final revision should not take you too long.

2. Find out about the exam

Find out:

* how many papers you have to sit
* how long each paper is
* how many questions you have to answer
* what choice of question there is
* on what basis the marks are allocated
* whether each question or each section is equally weighted
* whether more marks are given for some parts than others.

You may be able to find the details about the exams in your course handbook or in the subject outlines. Even if these documents give details of the exam, **always double check with your tutors** to ensure that the details are correct and that the exam format will be the same this year as it has been in previous years.

Type	Description	What it tests	Preparation
Essay based exams:	Answer 3-6 questions in several hundred words	Knowledge and understanding of subject + Ability to present evidence + Ability to express ideas logically and clearly + Recall of some of subject area (even for open book & open question)	Study old exam papers + Select revision topics + Make and learn summaries + Anticipate and practise questions
▨ Traditional	Questions unknown, no notes or materials allowed		
▨ Open book	Questions unknown, notes and materials allowed		
▨ Open question	Questions known, no notes or materials allowed		
Short answer exams	Answer a large number of questions with answers from one word to a paragraph in length	Recall of entire subject area	Read notes + Make and learn flashcards + Study old papers + Anticipate and practise questions
Multiple choice exams	Answer a large number of questions by selecting one response from a list of suggestions	Recall of specific detail of entire subject area	Learn fine details of notes + Study old papers + Anticipate and practise questions

Figure 8 Requirements for different types of exams.

3. Study old exam papers

Make a point of finding out how to get hold of old papers. Ask your tutors where you can find copies of previous papers. Check also whether your papers will follow the same format. Old exam papers may be available in the library. There may even be copies on the Intranet.

Your first look at a past exam paper may give you a bit of a fright. Don't panic when you read the questions. Almost every question is linked with something you have covered on the course. You just have to work out the link. Check:

▨ how the questions are set out on the page

▨ how many questions there are

▨ whether there are separate sections

▨ what kind of questions are set

▨ what sort of language is used

▨ whether there is an obvious relationship between the structure of the exam paper and the structure of the course; for example, if there is a question on each major section

4. Draw up a revision timetable

Write out a timetable and stick to it.

▨ Plan to start revising 6 to 8 weeks before your first exam.

▨ Fill in your timetable with a rough schedule showing how you plan to spend the time. This will help you focus on the size and the nature of the task.

▨ If each question carries the same marks, give equal time to the areas of the course that you have decided to revise.

▨ Space out your revision sessions. This is useful because it gives you practice at recall. At the beginning of each session, try to recall what you learnt at the previous session.

▓ Plan to work for a number of short sessions rather than long ones.

▓ Revise your weakest topic first.

▓ Set some time for practising exam questions.

5. Sort out your course materials

For each exam, make yourself a revision package of essays, projects, reports, exercises, notes on the topic and relevant course material. Label each package with the topic title and the study dates allocated to it. Don't gather together an enormous pile of books to read. It is too late now to do reading that should have been completed earlier. Be realistic about how much work you can get through in the time allowed.

6. Make time to go to revision classes

This is probably the time when attending tutorials is most useful. Classes make your revision easier and more pleasant. Group revision can be extremely efficient. It throws up all sorts of insights into problems and misinterpretations which might otherwise remain hidden. It also helps to sort out your ideas and offers many valuable clues and tips about how to approach the exam.

7. Form study groups with friends from the same course

Working with others helps to keep your own perceptions and plans within reasonable bounds. Revise together filling in gaps, helping each other out with problems and providing mutual support. Set each other questions to answer. Comment on and criticize each other's outline answers.

Divide up your class notes between the group. Write questions on the most examinable issues from each lecture. Photocopy the questions and outlined responses and then give a copy to the other members of the group. In this way you build up a bank of practice questions.

Specific techniques for different types of exams

Specific techniques for essay exams

Essay exams test understanding. You need to become familiar with the big picture rather than with the fine detail. With essay questions you need to know fewer facts and figures, but you are expected to connect the main points to make a coherent argument. Preparation for open book essay exams is almost the same as for traditional essay exams, since you can't spend too much time in the exam looking at your notes.

Make your revision an active process. Avoid simply rereading the same material over and over again. This is not only boring, it also misses the point. Revision for essay exams is not primarily a task of memorizing material. It is more like doing a jigsaw puzzle: you need to sort out the pieces and then fit them together to make the overall picture. This process of making connections and developing an overview is what you are required to do when answering questions in an exam. You need to be able to use what you know to argue a case which relates directly to the question. This requires a flexible understanding of the subject matter.

1. Select your revision topics
Successful students are strategic in their revision. Having

studied the exam requirements, they know how many topics to prepare. They revise only as much of the course as they need to answer the required number of questions, plus a safety margin. If a topic does not come up in quite the form expected, they still have enough material to select another question. They then give their full attention to revising the chosen areas very thoroughly. If no choice of questions is allowed, you need to revise everything.

2. Make summaries
Your aim when making summary notes is to end up with a set of short concise notes that outline the main themes and issues that you have identified from lectures and your reading.

- **Read through all the materials you have for a particular topic.** For example: lecture notes, notes from your reading, preparation for tutorials and seminars, assessed essays, comments on your assessed work, and so on.

- **Develop an overview and structure for the material.** As you read, relate the material to what you already know. Have a questioning approach. Concentrate on identifying the main themes and outlining the scope of the topic.

- **Pick out the key points.** You will probably have to work through a number of sets of 'summary' notes before you are able to make them concise enough. Essentially, with each draft you are making summaries of summaries. You don't want mounds of detail. Your aim is gradually to peel back the layers of the subject, until you end up with its basic skeleton.

- **Produce a single summary for each topic.** Mind maps (see Chapter 6) are a useful way of making these summary sheets, or you may prefer to use index cards.

- **Produce a single master summary which outlines the main subject matter for the whole section of the course.**

▓ **Learn your summaries.**

In following this process, you concentrate the broad themes and the detailed discussion of the course into a form which is much more manageable. In the exam, you reverse the process, moving from summaries to broad themes and discussions. You remind yourself of the topics on your master summary sheet, to identify what main topics relate to the question. You should then be able to recall your summary notes and so be able to reconstruct the body of the subject area.

3. Focus on questions
Try to predict the exam questions
In an exam, there is a limited number of topics on which questions can be asked. By studying the cycles and sequences of questions in old exam papers, you can get a **rough** guide to what past examiners thought were the important areas of the course. Revise old exam papers, note particularly any trends or similarities in the questions that have been set. If the same general issue has been the focus of two or three questions over the past few years, then emphasize it in your revision.

Don't, however, rely too much on predictions from old papers. Old papers have their uses, but should only form a part of your exam preparations. As well as looking at old papers, see if you can pick up hints from your tutors about topics they think are important.

Set your own questions
As you go through your notes, keep putting yourself in the position of the examiner. Ask yourself what sort of questions you would set on the various topics and draw up a list of possible questions. Exchange these lists with other students.

Analyse exam questions
For each question, you must be clear about what you have

to do. Look at the question word by word and make sure you know what each word means. If, in the exam, there is a term that you don't know, you will get very few marks if you guess and get it wrong. Look at how the words are arranged. Are you asked simply to describe something or are you also asked to explain it?

Identify the topic and process terms

Topic terms are the words dealing with the concepts which are the focus of the question. **Process terms** tell you what operations you are to carry out such as describe, critically analyse, trace the development of, evaluate, justify, etc (see Chapter 10).

Practise answering exam questions

This is a most useful exam preparation activity. Writing the answer to an exam question is similar to writing an essay. The difference is that you have to complete the essay much more quickly. You need to practise and develop a much more nimble style of essay writing to get yourself toned up for the exam. You may find it useful to reread Chapter 10 to remind yourself about the qualities of a good essay.

As you practise answering questions, you don't need to write out a full answer every time. Select a question from an old paper and then take about 10 minutes to sketch out an answer.

Examine each question carefully as outlined above. Decide:

▓ What is the question getting at?

▓ What point of view is the question presenting?

▓ Which section of the course does the question relate to?

▓ What themes, examples, evidence, ideas can you draw on from the course?

❋ What would be a good order to take the points in?

Devise a basic structure for your answer. Draw up a detailed plan with major and minor headings and paragraph themes. Check that you know what details to put under each section.

Find out how much you can write during the time allowed. From time to time, set yourself a timed answer to write under exam conditions. This is even better if done with other people. Compare what you covered in the timed essay with the earlier answer in note form. You may find that the timed essay covers only part of the material in the note form essay because you have overestimated how much you can write in the time allowed. You then need to prune your outline plan to fit the time available. Timed essay practice can prove invaluable in highlighting major timing problems.

Don't be discouraged if the answers you produce look unimpressive compared with your essays. Exam answers are judged roughly along the same lines as essays, but to much lower levels of expectation because of the constraints under which they are written. Discuss your efforts with other students, arrange to swap answers with them. In this way you will discover your strengths and weaknesses.

Techniques for short answer exams

Short answer exams test recall. Short answer papers demand less effort in the exam room than an essay exam, but they do demand a knowledge of the entire subject area. The questions frequently ask you to define critical terms or give an interpretation.

❋ **Become familiar with past exam papers.** In this way you will be able to recognize the kinds of questions that frequently occur.

▨ **Read your notes** with an eye specifically on those details which could be included in the exam.

▨ **Make lists of important definitions**, technical terms, important figures, issues you can summarize in a paragraph or two.

▨ **Make flash cards** with the term written on one side and the definition written on the other. On the front of each card write a term that you want to learn about and on the back add the definition or the major points that you want to remember. Prepare these cards following each lecture as you progress through the semester.

▨ **Learn the flashcards**. Carry them around with you and use them to test yourself, any time you have a few minutes to spare.

▨ **Practise answering questions.** Answer the question exactly. Don't give more information than the question requests. If your extra part is wrong you could lose marks. Don't waste time rewriting the question as part of your answer.

▨ **Set yourself a timed paper and complete it under exam conditions.**

Techniques for multiple choice exams

Multiple choice exams test recognition. In multiple choice exams you are expected to answer correctly by being able to recognize the most appropriate response from a list of suggestions.

▨ **Become familiar with the fine detail of your notes.** You need to memorize large numbers of facts and figures, but you are not expected to make connections between them.

▨ **Read and reread class notes** that you have supplemented with additions and corrections. Repeated readings of your notes will help to fix the broad themes and specific details in your mind.

▓ **Practise answering your own questions.** You may not be able to get access to past multiple choice exam papers. Because good multiple choice papers take a great deal of time to compile, they may well be reused and so copies are usually not distributed. Share your questions with others in your study group, so that you build up a large bank of possible questions.

Coping with exam anxiety

It is extremely unlikely that you will ever be totally free from stress when approaching examinations. In fact, a total lack of anxiety could result in your performing below your ability level. Anxiety can enhance your performance, but an excess of anxiety can paralyse you with panic. What you need to be able to do is to recognize and manage your stress, so that it does not become disruptive and interfere with your performance.

Surface the source of your anxiety
Knowing what has contributed to your anxiety is one of the most effective ways of coping with it. List the things about revision and exams that make you feel anxious. Take each one of the items on your list and answer the following questions:

▓ What has led to my having these feelings?

▓ How am I reacting physically?

▓ Is there anything I am doing which contributes to this situation?

▓ If someone else were in this situation, what would I advise them to do?

▓ What can I do over the next week to help the situation?

▓ Is my plan realistic?

Recognize your own signs of stress
There is a close relation between muscle tension and emotional states. Being able to recognize and release any unnecessary muscle tension helps avoid excess fatigue and protects the body against the effects of anxiety and stress. Learn to be aware of your levels of tension: for example, discomfort in your stomach, headache, knots in the back and neck. Once you have identified when and where in your body you feel tension, you can take steps to deal with it.

Use relaxation techniques
Find relaxation techniques that work for you and use them to reduce your tension. Ideally the best time to start learning and practising relaxation is some months before the exams. You could try yoga, meditation or relaxation tapes.

You could also try the following techniques which can be used on your own or in an exam room.

1. Breathe in until your lungs seem totally full and then take a sudden, quick extra breath through the mouth, before slowly breathing out. Repeat five or six times.

2. As you begin to feel tense, think to yourself (or say loudly) STOP! Clench your teeth and jaw, hold for the count of five. Repeat, tensing first your eyes and forehead, then your neck and shoulders and finally your hands and arms.

3. Take two or three deep breaths, letting them out as slowly as you can. Relax and drop your shoulders with a quiet sigh. Close your eyes and picture someone you care about saying something encouraging to you. Stay with that picture for a moment or two. Open your eyes.

Have confidence in yourself

Stress is often made worse by our own negative thoughts: _'I can't do this'_, _'I'm stupid'_, _'I'll fail'_. Learn to replace these negative thoughts with positive ones. For example: _'I will succeed'_, _'I'll get through with flying colours'_. At first you may not believe these messages, but over time they will sink in and have an effect.

Use positive visualization

Close your eyes. Relax, take a few slow deep breaths, breathing in for a count of five, hold for five and exhale for a count of five. Now visualize yourself succeeding in the exams. Imagine what it will be like seeing your high marks on the pass list; telling your friends and family; enjoying the benefits of your success. Repeat to yourself some of your positive statements. Develop the visualization each time you practise it.

Get things in proportion

While you don't want to approach the exam with the intention or expectation of doing any less than your best, it certainly is not worth turning your life into a nightmare over it. If you recognize the fact that you can survive the worst the exam can throw at you, namely failure, it will help you to keep things in proportion.

Keep in contact with your friends

Anxiety tends to be worse in students who shut themselves away from social contacts and try and study all day and most of the night.

Take some exercise

Do something that is fun

Don't give yourself a hard time for not being able to deal with your own stress.

Preparing for examinations: key points

▓ Match your preparations to the type of exam that you are taking.

▓ Learn to recognize your own symptoms of stress.

▓ Use relaxation techniques to reduce your anxiety.

---

14 Exams: the final countdown

This chapter explains:

▓ what to do the night before and morning of the exam

▓ how to complete different kinds of exams

▓ what to do after the exam

The night before the exam

The night before the exam is the time to make your final preparations for your big performance. If you have followed your revision plan, you should have covered all the necessary material. Now you need to take care of yourself, both physically and mentally, to ensure that you are in top form for your big day.

This is not the time to challenge your mind with new and difficult concepts. Most exams test not only what you know, but whether you can use the material you know. When you get tired and overstressed, your ability to use what you know falls off rapidly.

If you feel you want to do something, make it gentle revision. Keep to things you know well. Browse through your notes and run through the general issues in your mind.

Try to go to bed early enough so that you have a reasonable night's sleep. It is better to have a clear head than a few extra facts learnt the night before. Remember to set your alarm and allow yourself plenty of time to get ready in the morning.

Getting to sleep

You may find it difficult to get to sleep the night before the exam. If this happens, try the following relaxation exercise.

Focus on your breathing.

As you breathe in, visualize the number 100 in your mind.

Say 100 to yourself.

As you breathe out, trace the number with a finger tip, on the palm of your opposite hand.

Breathe in and visualize the number 99.

Repeat the process, counting backwards from 100.

Doing this exercise will preoccupy your mind. You won't have the opportunity to think of anything else, including the exam. Also by counting backwards from 100, you should bore yourself off to sleep!

The morning

▨ **Please yourself.** Whatever people tell you about what you should or shouldn't do on the morning of an exam, the important thing is to do what feels right for you. If you want to, get up early and go through your notes one more time, that's fine. If you don't want to look at your notes, that's also fine.

▨ **Stay positive.** Don't let your mind break off into thinking catastrophic thoughts. Displace any negative thoughts with a firm, positive, 'I can do it'.

▨ **Have a good breakfast.** Thinking actively for up to three hours is hard work. Hard work requires energy. Research evidence indicates that if you haven't eaten for some time, your concentration level will be reduced.

▓ **Organize your equipment.** Check to see that you have all you need for the exam: enrolment card; pens; pencils; ruler; calculator; any other special equipment that you need.

▓ **Set off with plenty of time to spare.** You will have checked the time and place of the exam well in advance. Allow enough time for your journey, with some to spare to allow for eventualities like the bus being late or the traffic being heavy.

Arriving at the venue

If you have followed the advice above, you should get to the right place, at the right time and in the right frame of mind. When you arrive, avoid the 'doom and gloom squad'. It is not at all helpful to risk depressing yourself by being negative at this stage. You will hardly notice when people are talking about things you do know, all you will hear is the things you didn't get done and your positive thinking will rapidly disappear.

Find a quiet corner away from the crowd. Go for a walk round the block, find a quiet seat in the library or even sit in the lavatory! Do anything to be on your own. Run through your major headings once more if you want to, or practise a positive visualization exercise (see Chapter 13).

In the exam room

There is no point in worrying once you get into the exam room. In fact once the exam has started you may actually find it quite exhilarating and challenging!

Get comfortable
When you take your place, check the physical conditions. You are going to be there for up to 3 hours, so you need to

be comfortable. Can you see properly? If you are in sunlight, ask for the blinds to be drawn. If it is too dark, ask for the lights to be put on. Does your desk wobble? Wedge something under it, to stop this.

Take your time

When you are told that you can turn over the exam paper, the temptation is to begin straight away. **Slow down!** It is **vital that you do not misread** what you are being asked to do. There will be plenty of time for you to work at speed once you have drawn up your work plan.

Read the instructions

This is **crucial to exam success**. Don't assume the format of the paper is the same as the past papers you have seen. The instructions to candidates may have changed. Most students have at some stage misread critical instructions: they answer too many questions; leave out compulsory ones; select from the wrong sections on the paper.

Read the instructions twice. The second time through underline any process words (see Chapter 10). Before you begin working on the paper, you need to ensure that you are going in the right direction. **Check:**

▓ how many questions in total you need to answer

▓ whether the questions carry equal marks

▓ if any questions are compulsory

▓ if there are different sections to the paper

▓ how many questions you have to answer from each section

▓ whether you have to write each answer in a separate answer booklet

By following this process, you should have a clear under-standing of exactly what you are required to do. What you do next depends on whether you are taking an essay, a short answer or multiple choice exam.

Essay exams

There are four stages involved in completing your answers to essay exam questions:

1. read

2. select

3. plan

4. write

1. Read

▨ **Read through all of the questions on the paper.**

▨ **Make a note against each question.** Indicate whether it is a probable (a tick), possible (a question mark), improbable (one cross) or impossible question (two crosses).

▨ **Read through the questions again.** Focus on the questions that are on the topics you prepared during your revision. Check whether your first evaluation was a correct one. You may now be able to convert a 'possible' into a 'probable'.

2. Select your questions

▨ **Underline parts of the question.** Underline the topic terms which tell you the concepts which are the focus of the question. Circle the process terms which tell you what operations you are to carry out. Doing this enables you to focus your attention on precisely what the question is ask-ing you to do.

▨ **Don't be put off a question just because the wording is different from what you expected.** The question on your revision topic may look more difficult simply because you know so much about the subject. Other questions may look easier because you don't know enough about the topic to realize their full implications. You are much more likely to produce a solid answer to one of your prepared topics, even if you feel unhappy with the question.

▨ **Don't try to impress the examiners by your question choice.** Don't tackle questions because you think they are important or because they seem difficult. Instead try to impress the examiner by answering questions well.

3. Plan

Plan your time
Spend time answering questions according to the marks they carry. Give equal time to questions that carry equal marks. The explanation for this is the law of diminishing returns: you get most marks in the first few minutes.

If a question is marked out of 20, it is relatively easy to get the first 5 marks, a bit harder to get the next 5, considerably harder to get the next 5 and next to impossible to get the final 5, even for your best answer. It is much easier to accumulate marks at the lower end of the scale, than at the upper end. Don't spend extra time on some questions, trying to write the 'perfect' answer to get those final few marks. You are unlikely to be successful. Spend roughly the same amount of time on each question, however weak you feel on some of them.

Work out a rough timetable
Allocate:

▨ 10 minutes for reading the paper and selecting your questions

▓ 5–10 minutes for planning each answer

▓ equal time to answer questions carrying equal weight

▓ 15–20 minutes for checking through your paper

For an exam paper that asks you to complete five, equally weighted essays in three hours, your plan may look something like this:

9.30–9.40	*Read paper and select questions*
9.40–10.15	*Plan and write answer for question 1*
10.15–10.35	*Plan answers to questions 2, 3, 4, 5 (see below)*
10.35–11.00	*Write answer to question 2*
11.00–11.25	*Write answer to question 3*
11.25–11.50	*Write answer to question 4*
11.50–12.15	*Write answer to question 5*
12.15–12.30	*Check through paper*
12.30	*Finish*

If you find that you are falling behind your timetable, draw your answer to a close as quickly as you can. Don't leave the question half finished in the hope that you will have time to come back and finish it. Not only will you have lost your train of thought, it is also unlikely that you will have any spare time, since you are already running late.

Plan your answers
Resist the urge to start writing straight away once you have selected your questions. Never start writing your answer without an outline plan. The examiner will expect a logical, well structured argument. The plan is your map. It will help you organize the structure of your answer. Planning

answers is also a good way of getting ideas down quickly on paper so you don't have to worry about them escaping your memory. Time spent planning is therefore time well spent. Allow between 5 and 10 minutes to plan your answer to each question.

Note down ideas

Even while reading the questions, if you have an idea write it down straight away. Some of these initial ideas could well be useful in triggering further thoughts, or in helping to structure your essay. Note down topics that might be relevant in answering the question. Don't worry about how to use the ideas yet. Keep rereading the question to help focus on what you are being asked to do.

If there is no scrap paper, use your exam booklet for making notes. Tear out the centre pages of the booklet if this is permitted. You will be able to have the plan in view as you write your answer. If this is not allowed, use the answer booklet instead. You can cross out your notes later.

Organize your ideas

Start with the headings: *introduction*, *body* and *conclusion*. Under each of these headings, write any ideas which you think are relevant. Sort out what to use and what to leave out. Keep rereading the question. Everything you write should have a clear relevance to the question. Don't include material just because you learnt it and want an opportunity to use it. You will lose marks rather than gain them if you give the impression that you are uncritically throwing course material before the examiner's eyes.

Plan all your answers in the first part of the exam

It is very hard to think straight in the final stages of the exam, when you are getting tired and you may be working against the clock. You may prefer to plan all of your answers before beginning to write any of them. Alternatively you may prefer to answer your best question first, to give you confidence and to allow you to relax into your stride. When you have completed one answer, you can plan the answers to all your other questions.

4. Write your answer

Write your answers following the plans that you have made.

▓ **Introduction:** this is strategically a very important section as it will establish a set of either positive or negative expectations in the mind of the marker. You need to start off very strongly and create a favourable impression. Tell the marker how your essay is organized and structured. Demonstrate that your answer is going to be clear, logical and well constructed.

▓ **Body:** you will only have a short time to write so try to organize the body with no more than three major sections. Keep a clear view of the question and try to generate three ideas or concepts which are logically related to each other.

▓ **Conclusion:** leave the reader with a positive impression of your work at the end. The conclusion should wrap up the essential features of your argument and move on to a statement of what you conclude. You might want to return to the question that you have been answering. Use phrases from the question to structure your conclusion so that it reflects what you were asked to do.

Rest between the questions

Take short rest breaks from four to six times during the exam. After finishing the first question in the exam, take a quick break to refresh yourself both mentally and physically. Put your pen down, stretch then close your eyes. Let your body relax and then focus on your breathing. As you breathe slowly in and out over the next three breaths, say to yourself *'relax'*. Then stretch again and go on with your next question.

Keep to your time plan

Remember the law of diminishing returns. Avoid writing at excessive length on the essay question that you know a great deal about. If you do write too much on some questions you will not have enough time for others. If, despite your time plan, you find you have no time left to finish the last question, at least write some notes about it in summary form.

Check your work

Most markers will be irritated by careless mistakes, misspellings, and grammatical errors. Read through your essay quickly and correct any errors so that your mark reflects the quality of your thinking, not the carelessness of hasty writing. **Check:**

▓ What you have written is exactly what you want to say.

▓ Your writing is reasonably legible. You are likely to be penalized if the examiner has difficulty in deciphering your handwriting. You may even be asked to pay to have your exam script typed out.

▓ You have recorded your details accurately.

If you have time, tidy up your script: underline headings; rule between sections.

Short answer exams

These exams are more straightforward than essay exams, but you still need to keep an eye on the time and check for errors.

When answering short answer questions be concise. Get right to the point, don't waffle. If necessary, use bullet points to cover any details which you believe to be essential to your answer.

Multiple choice exams

▓ When reading the questions, underline the key terms to focus your attention on the specific issues being addressed.

▓ Be exact in your interpretation of critical words such as *many, some, none, always, sometimes, never, more, less, best, least.* These words give specific meaning to the question content.

▓ Read all options before selecting the most appropriate answer. Remember that statements with words like *always* and *never* are less likely to be correct. The less restrictive the statement, the more likely it is to be correct.

▓ Do all the easy questions first; return to the more difficult ones for reconsideration.

▓ If you have been told there is no penalty for guessing then be certain that one answer is recorded for every question. If, on the other hand, guessing is penalized, then record an answer only if you can narrow it down to two possible choices.

▓ Do not make stray marks on the answer sheet.

▓ Check that the answer space number corresponds to the question number.

▓ Do not change an answer unless you know that the recorded answer is definitely wrong. Studies have shown your first answer is more likely to be correct, unless you remember some new information.

After the exam

Don't have a post mortem as these can be depressing. Everyone's approach is different and there is no sense in worrying after the event. You may well have several more exams to prepare for, perhaps on the following day, so you need to maintain a positive approach. Give yourself time to unwind.

When you have done this, spend a few minutes reviewing your performance in the last exam. See if it gives you any ideas for the next one. For example, if you ran out of time to do the final question, plan to manage your time better. Don't use the review period to blame yourself about the marks you may have lost.

Exam review classes

Exam papers are not usually returned to you after they have been marked. Tutors may, however, use class time to go through exam questions. Always attend these classes. They will help you understand how you gained or lost marks in the exam. This knowledge should help you improve your performance next time.

Exams: the final countdown: key points

▪ Read and follow the instructions on the exam paper very carefully.

▪ Read through all of the questions before you begin writing your answers.

▪ Check over your paper and make any final corrections.

▪ Review your performance after the exam, concentrating on what you can learn about taking exams in the future.

A Appendix A
The Dewey Decimal system of classification

Main divisions of Dewey Decimal classification:

000 General topics
100–199 Philosophy and Psychology
200–299 Religion
300–399 Social sciences
400–499 Languages
500–599 Pure sciences
600–699 Technology (applied sciences)
700–799 Arts (including recreation)
800–899 Literature
900–999 Geography, History and Biography

Each main division is then subdivided, for example:

300 Social sciences
310 Statistics
320 Political science

330 Economics

340 Law

350 Public administration

360 Social services

370 Education

380 Commerce

390 Custom and Folklore

Each subdivision is also subdivided into more specific topics, for example:

330 Economics

331 Labour economics

332 Financial economics

333 Land economics

334 Co-operatives

335 Socialism

336 Public finance

337 International finance

338 Production

339 Macroeconomics

Appendix B
The Library of Congress system of classification

The Library of Congress system has 21 main divisions, each given a letter of the alphabet. The following gives you a general idea of how the system works. Libraries do, however, modify this system according to their particular needs and requirements.

Main divisions of the Library of Congress system

A	Encyclopaedias and reference books
B	Philosophy, Psychology, Religion
C	Antiquities, Biography
D	History
E–F	American history
G	Geography, Anthropology
H	Social sciences, Economics, Sociology
I	Political science
K	Law
L	Education
M	Music

N   Fine arts

P   Language and Literature

Q   Science

R   Medicine and Health

S   Agriculture and Veterinary science

T   Technology

U   Military science

V   Naval science

Y   Statistics

Z   Books and Libraries, Bibliographies

Subdivisions are given another letter, for example:

Q   Science

QA   Mathematics

QB   Astronomy

QC   Physics

QD   Chemistry

QE   Geology

QH   Natural history

QK   Botany

QL   Zoology

QM   Anatomy

QP   Physiology

QR   Bacteriology

The letters are then followed by numbers to enable more subdivisions.

C Appendix C
Abbreviations and symbols to aid note making

Abbreviations

eg	for example
cf	compared with
ct	contrast
NB	note particularly
co	company
C19	19th century
&, +	and
b/w	between
@	at, each
re.	about, concerning, related to
p	page

Symbols

∴	therefore
∵	because

=	equals
≠	does not equal, is not the same as
→	leads to, causes, direction
↑	increase, much, elevated, high
↓	decrease, descend, low, little, few
↔	both ways, either way
>	greater or more than
<	less than
+	and
≈	approximately
#	number
Δ	change
%	per cent
⊃	implies, it follows from this that ...

Initials

EC	European Commission
H of C	House of Commons

Shorthand

u	you	mk	make
y	why	wl	will/well
r	are	dnt	don't
q	queue	fr	from
cn	can		

D Appendix D
Commonly
confused words

affect – to influence
effect – result, or, to get things done

alternate – coming one after the other by turns
alternative – giving a choice between things

contemptible – deserving of contempt
contemptuous – showing contempt for others

council – an assembly
counsel – advice, or to advise

dependant – a person who depends on another
dependent – depending on someone or something else

disinterested – impartial
uninterested – having no interest in

eligible – fit to be chosen, qualified
illegible – unreadable

honourable – worthy of honour
honorary – given as an honour; done without payment

imply – to signify
infer – to draw a conclusion from

militate – to work or operate against
mitigate – to lessen, moderate or make less severe

practical – having to do with practice
practicable – capable of being put into practice

principal – chief
principle – a rule of conduct

seasonal – having to do with a season
seasonable – suitable to the season

E Appendix E Common grammatical errors

Only change tense if you have a good reason for doing so
The tense used in a piece of writing can jump from past to future to present with no apparent logic. When writing, select one tense and stick to it.

Use the active voice rather than the passive
It makes your writing shorter and more direct and so helps clarity. For example:

> *The student is spoken to by the tutor.*   (passive)
>
> *The tutor speaks to the student.*   (active)

Avoid ambiguity
This can arise in a number of ways. The following are some of the most frequent causes of ambiguity:

▒ The incorrect positioning of a work or phrase:

> *No unnecessary force was used to put an end to the disturbance by the police.*
>
> *He met his former girlfriend out walking with his wife.*

▒ The use of words with a double meaning or more than one meaning:

> *The new secretary worked very happily under the export manager.*

▨ The misuse of punctuation:

Jim took his wife and his dog on a lead for a walk in the park. This sentence needs a comma after the word *wife.*

Use apostrophes correctly
The apostrophe is used:

▨ to show the omission of letters and figures:

> *can't* (cannot), *it's* (it is), *the early '20s*

▨ with 's' to form the plural of letters, numbers, symbols and words which do not have a plural form or are not easily recognizable as plurals:

> *1's, 2's, 5's, p's* and *q's, do's* and *don'ts*

▨ to form the possessive case of nouns. In the singular the apostrophe is placed before the s:

> *the student's book, the lecturer's notes*

in the plural, the apostrophe is placed after the s:

> *the Students' Union, the lecturers' staff room*

▨ with expressions involving time, the apostrophe is used after the s:

> *Two weeks' time, three months' holiday*

▨ always where the letter is missed out, for contractions,:

> *don't* (do not); *weren't* (were not); *wouldn't* (would not); *they're* (they are); *who's* (who is).

Do not use an apostrophe with the following personal pronouns: *its, hers, ours, theirs, yours.* The single exception is *one's.*

If you can't think of a reason for an apostrophe, DON'T use one.

Index